1983

REAGANOMICS

N

COPYRIGHT © 1983 By WEST PUBLISHING CO.
50 West Kellogg Boulevard
P.O. Box 3526
St. Paul, Minnesota 55165

Library of Congress Cataloging in Publication Data

Kimzey, Bruce W.
 Reaganomics
 Includes index.
 1. Supply-side economics I. Title
HB241.K54 1983 338.973 82-24750
ISBN: 0-314-73187-3

REAGANOMICS

Bruce W. Kimzey

University of Nevada, Reno

WEST PUBLISHING COMPANY

St. Paul   New York   Los Angeles   San Francisco

CONTENTS

PREFACE

The question most frequently asked of economists during the past two years has probably been, "What is Reaganomics?" It was usually followed by a series of questions on goals, programs, feasibility, and the future of the president's plan. Whether the questions arose in classes, luncheon speeches, or in business seminars, I was also usually asked why no one had taken the time to write a simple and direct explanation of what President Reagan was attempting to do. I decided that it was time for someone to undertake this assignment.

This short work is intended to answer the major questions about Reaganomics. I believe that people must understand the historical circumstances the president inherited if they are to understand why he turned to a different theory and policy approach to solving economic problems. I have attempted to provide a straightforward and simple explanation of the theory, which is needed to understand the president's program. Finding the appropriate theoretical balance is always difficult, but I have tried to error on the side of too little rather than too much.

It has not been my intent to attempt to justify and apologize for the president's program, or to criticize and condemn it. While my personal philosophy is sympathetic to the goals of the plan, the program presented could never have accomplished all of its goals, and certainly not in the time period proposed by

Reagan. I agree with Nobel laureate George Stigler who recently said that if he were required to grade Reaganomics he would have to assign an incomplete. It is too early to pass final judgment on a program that has accomplished some of its goals, failed in others, and perhaps helped create some new problems in the process.

This book is directed toward two separate groups. The first is students in any undergraduate macroeconomics class including principles, intermediate theory, public finance, or money and banking, or in graduate classes. Since the book concentrates on policy rather than theory, it could provide the basis for discussion at any level.

The second group is interested and informed laypeople affected by public policy and wanting a better understanding of what is happening and what the future may bring. This group includes those in business, finance, education, and politics who have an interest in and some prior exposure to economic theory and want a brief explanation of the president's program.

I am indebted to many people for encouragement and suggestions in preparing this work, especially those who asked enough questions to force me to think through the logic of Reaganomics and to do the reading and research required to present informed answers. I am also indebted to those who have read and commented on early drafts of the manuscript. Their suggestions have helped me avoid many errors and also clarify many arguments. I would like to thank Dr. Otis Gilley, University of Texas, Austin; Dr. Dale Truett, University of Texas, San Antonio; Dr. Robert Pulsinelli, Western Kentucky University; Dr. Robert Carson, SUNY, Oneonta; and Dr. Douglas McMillan, University of Kentucky, for review comments and suggestions. A special thanks to Dr. Tom Cargill of the University of Nevada, Reno for his encouragement and suggestions throughout the preparation of the manuscript. As usual, the final responsibility for the work rests with the author.

1 WHAT DID REAGAN INHERIT?

With the possible exception of Franklin Delano Roosevelt, no American president in modern history can match the success of Ronald Reagan in changing the direction of the federal government's economic policy during his first two years in office. Reagan's success in convincing Congress to approve his proposals for massive tax and expenditure cuts has surprised even his most avid supporters. In addition, just as FDR's New Deal programs became synonymous with government expansion, the new Reagan economic program has come to mean sizable, even devastating, cuts in virtually all nondefense expenditures.

President Reagan was elected as a fiscal conservative who promised to cut taxes, expenditures, government regulation, inflation, interest rates, and unemployment. Yet in less than two years his programs to implement these promises have become the center of the greatest controversy over economic policy since the Great Depression. His programs of "Reaganomics" mean almost as many different things to voters as there are different voters. Even economists have not yet fully comprehended the potential impacts of such a major policy shift.

But the president's economic program was not developed in a vacuum, without theory, precedent, or expectations. It is a fairly logical combination of his conservative background and bits and pieces of several economic theories, but supported by limited economic experience and policies of the past. But the failures of the economic program of the Carter administration and its predecessors, and the frustrations over an expanding and increasingly insensitive and unresponsive federal bureaucracy, led voters to turn to Reagan in the fall of 1980.

President Reagan inherited an economy with a number of serious problems. Inflation and high interest rates were the major concerns, but unemployment, energy shortages, high taxes, and falling productivity also demanded immediate attention by the president and his economic policy advisors. Attempts by previous administrations to deal with these problems had been unsuccessful at best, and some critics argued that policy had created some problems in the unsuccessful attempts to solve others. But the Reagan program, which places emphasis on reducing inflation and the size of the government sector, has been blamed for the 1981-82 recession and the existence of the highest rate of unemployment since the Great Depression. In addition, the president's expressed goals of expanded savings, investment, and business confidence have not been met. Indeed, by the summer of 1982 confidence in the economy and the president's program was decreasing rather than increasing. Critics were arguing that the president's goal of lowering the inflation rate was being reached at a cost in unemployment and misery that was far too great.

Just as President Reagan's economic policies were a response to the apparent failures of earlier years, the policies of the 1960s and 1970s were generated in response to apparent failures of even earlier periods. Most economists recognize 1929 and the period of the Great Depression as the breaking point between the classical and Keynesian policy periods. In the pre-1929 period the market economy was believed to be inherently stable and self-correcting, so a minimum of government intervention was required, and then only to promote competition in the marketplace. The Federal Reserve System had been created in 1913 for the purpose of improving and promoting monetary stability, as well as bank liquidity and safety. Almost everyone agreed that the federal government budget should be balanced and expenditures and taxes be kept to a minimum.

The Great Depression brought with it a far-reaching loss of faith in the ability of the market to maintain full employment, even in the long run. In a four-year period the unemployment rate reached almost 25 percent and the nation's output of goods and services was cut in half. Banks and businesses failed by the thousands, and a period of pessimism and distrust of market forces replaced the optimism of the 1920s.

Federal Reserve monetary policy in the 1930s consisted primarily of increasing bank reserves in an effort to provide liquidity for expanding loans and creating jobs and output. But when businesses did not borrow to invest, banks were left with idle reserves. Most economists and politicians concluded that monetary policy was inadequate to raise the economy from such a depression.

In addition to an apparently ineffective monetary policy, the Hoover administration responded to falling federal revenues by increasing taxes and cutting expenditures. The economy simply sank lower into the depression.

In the depths of the depression an English economist named John Maynard Keynes published a revolutionary work, *The General Theory of Employment, Interest, and Money.*[1] The *General Theory*, as it came to be known, proposed a new role for government and the federal budget. In place of classical policies Keynes proposed the federal government take an active role in creating jobs and stimulating the economy through tax cuts and increases in spending. Keynes argued that the market was inherently unstable, tending toward a position of equilibrium at less than full employment. He also viewed monetary policy as ineffective, and competitive markets could not by themselves produce a sustained economic recovery. The budget was seen as a key to control of the aggregate demand for goods and services. Aggregate demand is the total demand from consumption spending by households, investment spending by business, and the government's purchase of goods and services. Consumption (and, to a more limited extent, investment) could be expanded by tax cuts, and, if combined with government spending increases, total demand would expand. Such budget policy was called *fiscal policy* and required increases in spending to solve a problem of insufficient or inadequate demand (such as existed during the Depression). It also required decreases in spending to solve a problem of excess demand (inflation). But a depression policy also resulted in budget deficits when government spending was increased and taxes were cut. Such deficits were argued to be a desirable and necessary part of the fight to reduce unemployment and expand the economy.

A side effect of Keynesian theory was an increase in government regulation of business, especially banking, and a decrease in the perceived ability of the Federal Reserve authorities to control the level of demand. Thus, fiscal policy began to replace monetary policy as the primary tool in the fight against unemployment and inflation. But Keynes was clearly more concerned with the unemployment problem, and inflation policy simply followed as a logical result of the theory. Even President Roosevelt used only limited fiscal policy stimulus, and thus the Depression was not really ended until the expansion that resulted from World War II when government spending rose from $14 billion in 1940 to over $96 billion by 1944. As a consequence, the unemployment rate fell to 1.2 percent. The government controlled inflation by wage and price controls rather than by an attempt to use either monetary or fiscal policy.

At the end of the war Congress passed the Employment Act of 1946, which stated the national goals of reaching and maintaining full employment and price stability. The act further charged the president and Congress with developing the necessary policies and programs to accomplish these goals. Full employment was then defined as a goal of 4 percent unemployment. This act became the guide and the justification for much of the fiscal policy programs of the next thirty years.

The 1950s were generally years of passive, rather than active, economic policy. Budget deficits resulted primarily from recessions or from forecasting failures rather than a deliberate policy of the Eisenhower administration to use the budget to stimulate demand and control employment. Unemployment averaged about 5 percent during these years, and except for the inflation in 1951 induced by the Korean War, average price increases during the 1950s were only 1 to 2 percent a year.

The first real attempt to implement an active Keynesian policy in the United States is generally conceded to be the Kennedy tax cut of the early 1960s. An $11.5 billion tax cut was proposed to stimulate consumption and investment spending and is generally regarded as a major cause of the sustained growth and full employment of the mid-1960s. However, when the Johnson administration introduced its Great Society in 1964 and greatly expanded the war in Vietnam in 1965, government spending rose very rapidly and inflation became an economic issue. When the Keynesian prescription of budget surpluses to fight inflation proved to be less acceptable politically than the earlier deficits had been, inflation accelerated and the theoretical symmetry of Keynesian policy vanished.

The increased government spending in the 1960s, combined with the private spending expansion created by the 1964 tax cut, caused prices to begin rising by 1965. When President Johnson asked Congress for a tax increase in the form of a surcharge in 1966, congressional leaders refused unless it was accompanied by a reduction in spending. When Johnson refused to jeopardize either the Great Society or the Vietnam War effort, the fiscal policy inflation program bogged down. In its place a new emphasis was placed on monetary policy as an anti-inflationary tool. The Federal Reserve responded with a tight money policy, driving interest rates up and creating a series of credit crunches, the first two of which occurred in 1966 and 1969.[2]

The increase in interest rates, combined with Federal Reserve restrictions on interest that banks and other financial institutions could pay on savings, resulted in a process of *disintermediation* where savers removed funds from financial institutions and placed them directly in higher yielding investments, such as Treasury bills and stocks and bonds. This disintermediation process put great pressure on the stability of financial institutions but did not solve the inflation problem. Furthermore, as credit tightened, unemployment increased and the Federal Reserve was pressured to loosen credit restrictions and allow interest rates to fall.

The experience of the credit crunches also served to increase the debate between Keynesian policymakers and a growing body of economists called Monetarists, led by Professor Milton Friedman of the University of Chicago. Monetarists argued that the Federal Reserve should follow a policy of directly controlling the money supply rather than indirectly influencing money through control of interest rates. For example, a decrease in the money supply would decrease spending directly and, hence, cause inflation to decline. Keynesians argued that low interest rates would stimulate borrowing and increase the money supply and aggregate spending (demand), while high interest rates would decrease borrowing, the money supply, and spending.

Monetarists argued that interest rates were determined by market forces and could be influenced by the Federal Reserve only in the short run. Other factors, such as private investment and saving, the size of the federal deficit (and federal borrowing), and the expectations of future inflation, also influenced market interest rates. Thus, high interest rates could be associated with an increasing money supply as often as with a decreasing money supply. And since it was the growth in the supply of money that determined the rate of inflation, an interest rate policy was an ineffective long-run inflation tool.

During the 1970s it became increasingly difficult for monetary and fiscal authorities to deal effectively with the problems of inflation and unemployment. Control of inflation seemed to become the primary responsibility of the Federal Reserve, while a reduction in unemployment became the goal of fiscal authorities. But both problems worsened consistently throughout the decade.

Whenever unemployment increased, Congress responded with even bigger deficits and more government programs. Armed with the accepted Keynesian justification for deficits as an unemployment weapon, Congress created and expanded programs and spending at an unprecedented rate. At the same time, monetary authorities were pressured to allow a corresponding monetary expansion so total spending could rise and the unemployment rate could be reduced. Hence, monetary policy in the 1970s was designed primarily to accomodate an expansionary fiscal policy, while at the same time, Federal Reserve authorities were expected to use interest rates to control inflation. This conflict became increasingly serious throughout the decade. Two additional periods of credit crunch in 1974-75 and again in 1979-80 resulted when inflation increased during these periods and the Federal Reserve responded with high interest rates.

Until October 1979 there was a growing conflict in the use of Federal Reserve policy, with the money supply often growing at rapid rates, while interest rates were held high by Treasury borrowing and the Federal Reserve emphasis on interest rates as their anti-inflationary policy target. However, in October 1979 the Federal Reserve announced a major change in policy and began using money supply growth as the primary policy target. Since that time, policy has been more consistently restrictive, with some easing in the fall of 1982. The Federal Reserve's unwillingness to continue to finance federal deficits with an expanding money supply put additional upward pressure on interest rates during 1980-81 and contributed significantly to creating the recession that began in the late summer of 1981.

Also during the 1960s and 1970s Americans turned to the public sector for solutions to all economic problems. As a consequence, new programs to eliminate misery and inequity such as the War on Poverty, Community Development, Equal Employment Opportunity, Medicaid, and housing and education subsidies were created and grew rapidly. Critics have labeled this period as one in which Congress seemed to believe any problem could be solved if only enough programs were created and enough money spent. The economic programs of the period focused on attempts to create greater equality by increasing incomes and opportunities for the poor and racial minorities while also directly relieving economic burdens on such groups as the poor and the elderly. The Social Security system became the largest single government program financed by the fastest growing tax in the system, but programs such as food stamps, Medicaid, and housing assistance also grew rapidly. The result was an expanding budget that grew from $94 billion in 1960 to $196 billion in 1970, and then to $577 billion by 1980.[3]

One result of the expanding budget was an expanding federal bureaucracy and increased government regulation. Major new agencies, such as the Environmental Protection Agency (EPA) and the Occupational Safety and Health Administration (OSHA), new initiatives provided by Affirmative Action and Equal Employment Opportunity, and new cabinet formations like the Department of Energy and the Department of Education expanded government control and regulation in virtually every direction. One result was a growing concern that government was doing too much for vested interests while creating problems and unnecessary interference with the marketplace.

When the inflation of the period combined with the progressive income tax to increase tax revenues automatically, Congress expanded programs and expenditures even faster, until the $5 to $10 billion deficits in the 1960s became the $25 to $40 billion deficits in the 1970s. Even then the new government programs and expenditures failed to solve the problem of unemployment, and the decade of the 1970s became the decade of stagflation—the combination of inflation and unemployment—with economic policy increasingly a cause rather than a solution to economic problems.

High rates of inflation, combined with long-run expectations of continued high or rising inflation rates also led to a decrease in the real rate of return to savings, which contributed to high and rising interest rates. Inflationary expectations led consumers and businesses to spend rather than save since the value of savings and interest returns was expected to decrease over time. The result was decreased savings and increased borrowing, which put even more upward pressure on interest rates. In addition, lenders built inflation into their interest calculations and required higher and higher market interest in an effort to maintain a constant real value of their assets over time. By the end of the 1970s, high interest rates were recognized as a major economic problem creating problems of credit allocation and increasing the real costs of business investment, while also putting new burdens on family budgets.

The combination of decreased saving, tight money, and rising interest rates also had an adverse effect on business investment. With decreased funds available (and government taking a rising share of what was available) and an increasing cost of investment funds, businesses tended to postpone investment in all but the most profitable projects. Businesses also tended to favor short-term debt over long-term debt, hoping that high interest rates would be temporary and existing debt could be refinanced at lower long-term rates at some future date. One of the industries hit hardest by such a market was obviously housing and construction, which relies so heavily on the existence of favorable long-run credit availability. When interest rates increased and funds decreased, families stopped buying new houses, construction activity decreased rapidly, and the industry slumped into a major depression by 1980.

Falling investment, combined with high inflation, interest rates, and the costs of government regulation, had the indirect impact of reducing the rate of growth in labor productivity. Productivity is defined as output per hour worked and has historically increased at an average annual rate of about 3 to 4 percent. That rate began to fall during the mid-1970s and actually became negative in the 1978-80 period. In other words, the average worker produced less value during each hour worked in 1980 than in 1977. One result of falling productivity when combined with increasing wages was an even greater pressure on business to increase prices. If business must pay higher wages for less output, profits will fall unless sales revenue expands—by either expanding volume or by raising prices. Thus, an important part of any inflation control program is an attempt to increase labor productivity or to decrease the rate of growth in wages. It is generally recognized that labor productivity will most likely respond to an increase in capital equipment available to workers (an increase in investment). Thus, a part of President Reagan's program has been an attempt to expand business investment in new plant and equipment.

A major new economic problem surfaced in late 1973 with the OPEC oil embargo. Combined with the Nixon administration price controls on gasoline, the embargo created a severe gasoline shortage. Near the end OPEC quadrupled the price of crude oil and put tremendous upward pressure on gasoline prices. As the Nixon price controls were relaxed, the price of all oil and gas products increased substantially. A new round of

OPEC price increases in 1979-80 again increased gasoline prices and contributed to general inflation. The shortages increased the focus on the long-term energy problems of the country, and the resulting price increases for all energy products and services compounded the inflation problems created by budget misman-agement and contributed directly to two different periods of re-cession before the decade was over. The government's response was the creation of a new Department of Energy with sweeping powers of regulation and significant new budgets to solve energy problems and to fight higher levels of unemployment.

Finally, the inflation of the 1960s and the 1970s also focused attention on a tax problem for individuals commonly called *tax bracket creep.* The major federal tax is the personal income tax, which uses a graduated or progressive rate structure; as an indi-vidual taxpayer's income increases so does the marginal tax rate. For example, a married couple with taxable income of $10,000 in 1980 would have paid $1,062 in taxes, with the last dollars of income taxed at a rate of 18 percent. Another couple with a $20,000 taxable income would have paid over three times as much ($3,225), with the last dollars taxed at a marginal rate of 24 percent. The largest incomes, those over $215,000, would have been taxed at a 70 percent marginal rate. Since incomes tend to rise during an inflationary period, taxpayers find them-selves in higher and higher brackets with the tax taking larger and larger shares of their extra dollars.

Tax bracket creep means that workers who get a 10 percent wage increase during a period of 10 percent inflation are actu-ally worse off in terms of real disposable income. It also means that the tax revenues of the federal government rise even faster than the inflation rate. As a consequence, government was ac-cused of being a major beneficiary of, and a major creator of, continual inflation. At the very least, tax bracket creep de-creased the incentives for government officials to reduce infla-tion. It also created a general attitude of frustration with the tax system, with most families feeling cheated over their rising tax burdens while expanded government programs seemed to provide assistance to an increasing number of people viewed as undeserving. One result was a tax revolt aimed primarily at local governments, but which extended to a general feeling that government at all levels was taking too much and doing too much for too many at too high a cost.

What did Reagan inherit? When he took office he faced: (1) the most persistent and serious inflation rate in this century, (2) the highest level of real interest rates in the nation's history, (3) a high and persistent level of unemployment, (4) the lowest rate of personal saving in the post-war period, (5) a stagnant economy with a low level of private investment and a high level of pessimism in the business community, (6) a falling level of labor productivity, (7) increasing concern over energy and other shortages, (8) a government sector increasing both its absolute and its relative size, (9) a rapidly expanding government bureaucracy and regulation of business, and (10) a rising taxpayer's revolt against high taxes.

Ronald Reagan campaigned on a platform of tax and expenditure reductions, a promise to increase defense spending, and a pledge to decrease government regulation. His Economic Recovery Program was a plan to emphasize private sector incentives and to decrease public sector size and market interference. While the president did not anticipate a major recession just as his program was being passed and implemented, the overall goals of the program were consistent with his campaign pledges. If the president's program had a major fault, it seems to be that it was overly optimistic and based primarily on the hope that the business community would respond to the incentives built into the program. Unfortunately, the expected optimism was delayed by the 1981 recession, and the confidence and rising expectations that the president counted on so heavily have not materialized in the first two years of his program.

2 THE LOGIC OF REAGANOMICS

"Reaganomics" is the term used to describe the entire Reagan administration program of economic recovery and reduction of the role of government but is most often associated with the president's tax and spending reduction programs. His proposals to reduce social welfare spending and increase defense expenditures are a combination of his own conservative background and traditional Republican theory on control of inflation. The tax reduction program is the result of the president's conversion to what economists call *supply-side* economic theory, with particular emphasis on the *Laffer curve* arguments for tax rate changes. The president has also encouraged the Federal Reserve to follow the monetary control program of the Monetarists.

While Reagan has openly embraced the supply-side and Monetarist theories as an integral part of his economic recovery plan,[1] two additional economic theories are sometimes used to help explain the president's program. While they have not been made a public part of the plan, the theories of *rational expectations* and the *natural unemployment rate* are both related to the Monetarist's arguments against an active fiscal policy to control short-run unemployment and inflation, and also seem to be consistent with the president's actions. Since all of these theories represent a departure from those used by earlier administrations, they can help explain why Reaganomics is viewed as a new approach to the use of economic policy and the role of government.

Supply Management and the Laffer Curve

For the past forty years the principle theoretical basis for governmental budget policy has been the theory of *demand management* proposed by Keynes in the 1930s. During the 1940s and 1950s budget policy was largely passive in that budget deficits and surpluses were not planned in advance for purposes of regulating the flow of total demand. The Kennedy tax cut, finally passed in 1964, represented the first attempt at active budget policy, designed to stimulate aggregate demand by a large, planned budget deficit created through a tax cut on personal and corporate incomes. (Ironically, this demand management tax cut also provided the basis for arguing that tax cuts will also stimulate aggregate supply.) Since the 1964 tax cut, expansionary budget policy has been used actively to stimulate demand. Unfortunately, the opposite policy of demand contraction through budget surpluses was not used, and budget or fiscal policy became synonymous with government expansion, deficits, and inflation.

The apparent unwillingness of budget authorities to use fiscal policy as a two-edged sword led many economists in the 1970s to reexamine the wisdom of using fiscal policy as a short-run stabilization tool. Some began to advocate balancing the full employment budget in an effort to achieve long-run stability of incomes and prices. The full employment budget assumed that the economy was operating at full employment and then projected the level of government revenues that would be available if the economy were really operating at that level. That amount of projected revenue was then proposed as a limit to government spending. But a balanced full employment budget generally still meant a large actual budget deficit, and when inflation and unemployment both increased, even the full employment budget was allowed to be in deficit. This mythical budget was seen by most as a useful policy planning tool but was certainly not an effective limit to government spending or the inflation that followed.

In this setting a small group of economists began to argue that demand management as a practical budget policy would not work. In its place they proposed to use the budget to manage the amount of aggregate supply—the total value of goods and services available in the marketplace. For example, if inflation is caused by an excess of total demand over total supply of goods and services available, then an alternative solution to reducing the amount of total demand would be to increase the supply of goods and services available to satisfy the demand. A side benefit to the plan would be that, instead of depressing the economy to reduce demand, the levels of investment, output, production, and income could be increased, creating a more healthy, stable, and growing economy. The major weapon in the supply-side program was seen as a tax policy designed to promote economic growth.

The ability of tax policy to create positive supply-side incentives has long been recognized by both economists and politicians, but the theory has been given new importance as an alternative to Keynesian demand management. The leading spokesmen for the supply-side theory are Dr. Arthur Laffer of the University of Southern California; Jude Wanniski, once a staff writer for the *Wall Street Journal* and now an economic consultant; and Paul Craig Roberts, a *Wall Street Journal* associate editor and a former assistant secretary of the Treasury for President Reagan.[2]

Supply-side theory contains two major propositions. First, cuts in tax rates should be used to increase private sector incentives to invest and produce, and therefore increase the total supply of goods and services available. Second, the United States and the rest of the world should return to use of the gold standard as a means of limiting the growth in the money supply and controlling inflation. Supply-siders decided early that the tax cut proposals should receive first attention because they had the greatest chance for political success and would lay the foundation for the eventual return to the gold standard.

According to popular legend, Dr. Laffer was sitting in a hotel restaurant sometime in the mid-1970s and began drawing diagrams on a napkin. In the process he developed a curve that has come to be called the Laffer curve, which forms the major theoretical basis for supply-side tax policies. A direct outgrowth of his supply-side orientation, Laffer's curve implies that high tax rates destroy incentives to produce and force production out of the mainstream economy and into what economists call the *underground* economy, thereby reducing the total tax base. At high existing tax rates, raising rates further may thus result in an actual decrease in tax collections, while cutting tax rates may lead to an increase in collections. The Laffer curve is shown in the figure on the following page. It is actually a backward-bending supply curve, where leisure is a substitute for work at very high wages (or tax rates, in this case).

According to Laffer's curve, a zero tax rate will yield zero tax revenue. This is obviously true since tax revenue is found by multiplying the tax rate (R) by some tax base (B). Therefore, a rate of zero percent will yield no revenue. The most common tax base is personal income, but taxes other than the federal income tax use a base of property value, consumption expenditures, or some measure of production or output. In each case, as the tax rate begins to increase, the revenues collected should also begin to rise. Laffer's argument is that as tax rates are raised from zero, taxpayers will work harder to recover the income lost to the tax, so the base will also increase (or at least remain constant) as the rate increases, so revenues will also rise.

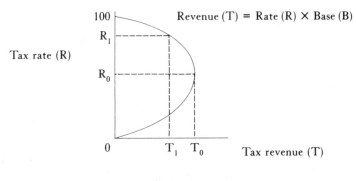

Laffer's Curve

But Laffer also argues that as the tax rate continues to rise, taxpayers become discouraged, and their willingness to work harder and produce more (or to report what is produced) in the face of rising taxes begins to decrease. As a result, it takes larger and larger increases in the tax rate to offset the declining tax base. At some point (R_0) the tax system will yield its maximum revenues (T_0) to the government, and further rate increases will create such large decreases in production and work incentives that revenue will actually fall. At a rate of R_1 revenues will have fallen to T_1. At the extreme case of a 100 percent tax rate, the only production that will take place will be in the underground economy where income goes unreported for tax purposes. The tax base will therefore be decreased to zero. A 100 percent rate multiplied by a zero base then yields zero revenues. It is important to note that the revenue maximizing rate R_0 is not necessarily—nor is likely to be—a 50 percent tax rate.

The policy conclusion from Laffer's curve is that a tax cut will actually lead to an increase in tax collections (assuming, of course, that the current rate is R_1, above the optimum rate of

R_0). A decrease in tax rates will lead to an increase in the incentives for taxpayers to work and produce since they will keep a larger share of the income they earn. In addition, any production and income that has been unreported as part of the underground economy will also surface and become part of the tax base. Laffer thus became the major advocate of tax decreases as a means for stimulating production and increasing the tax base. Politicians looking for a justification for either tax cuts or spending increases were obviously open to this type of proposal since it provides a theoretical argument for cutting taxes, while also increasing tax revenues and funds available to expand expenditures. One could therefore argue that it was possible to cut taxes, raise spending, and still not increase the budget deficit. The Laffer curve was clearly a popular political concept.

Professional economists, however, have not reacted as favorably as politicians to the Laffer curve proposals.[3] A number of questions and objections have been raised. For example, the curve is extremely difficult to test emperically to see if it is true. Even Laffer would not argue that a cut in tax rates would lead to an instantaneous increase in revenues. It takes some time to create new investment and production incentives and for new income and tax revenues to be raised. Even critics of the Laffer curve accept the fact that tax cuts stimulate production and income—but not enough to create an increase in total tax revenues. If taxes after one year are equal to previous projections without a cut, has the theory been proved or disproved? What about two years or three years later? Many forces work on the tax system, and the incentives to produce more or less and to measure the size of the underground economy are probably the most difficult of these forces to measure.

Consider other questions: Is there a separate Laffer curve for every individual taxpayer or one curve for the entire taxpaying population? Is there a separate curve for every tax or one curve that includes the total of rates for all different taxes paid? Does

the tax rate used to construct a curve include the rate of inflation as an indirect form of tax rate? How one answers these
questions will determine whether or not the total tax rate is
above or below the optimum, and whether or not a tax cut
would move the system toward or away from the optimum. The
optimum rate would be at a different level for each taxpayer if
everyone has a separate curve. And finally, if the curve includes
all rates, one tax may need to be cut substantially in order for
the overall tax rate to be cut a few percentage points. Laffer and
his supply-side colleagues have not provided adequate answers to
these kinds of questions, and hence most economists remain skeptical of the ability of the theory to provide the promised benefits.

It is important to note that Laffer argues for a cut in the
marginal tax rates and not in the average or *effective* rates. Marginal rates are those that apply only to the last, or marginal,
dollar of income earned. For example, the federal personal income tax rates in 1980 were graduated from 14 to 70 percent.
Individuals with low incomes paid only 14 percent of their taxable income (after deductions and exemptions) in tax. Those
with very large taxable incomes, those over $100,000, paid 14
percent of the first $500, but 70 percent of the last dollars
earned. A cut in the top bracket rate from 70 to 50 percent
would reduce the taxes of only the wealthiest taxpayers and
would not reduce their average tax rate in the same fashion,
since only a few of their income dollars were being taxed at the
highest rates.

Laffer argues that by cutting the highest, most burdensome,
marginal rates, the wealthiest taxpayers who have income subject to those rates would receive a substantial incentive to save,
invest, and earn more income since they would be able to keep
more of any additional dollars earned.

Few economists would argue with the contention that consumption and saving patterns vary with the level of income,
with saving an increasing function of income. The wealthy save

a much larger fraction of their income than do the poor. That is, an individual earning $5,000 a year may actually spend more than $5,000. Someone earning $20,000 a year may save $500, while another individual earning $100,000 may save $20,000. In each case the percentage of income saved increases as income increases. Thus, the major theoretical arguments were laid for the president's proposal to cut marginal income tax rates substantially, giving the major reductions to upper income individuals who would have the greatest incentives to save and to expand production and output.

While many economists recognize the truth in the arguments that reducing high marginal rates will increase saving and investment, it is not as obvious that the additional production and income generated by that saving and investment will yield enough new tax revenue to offset the revenue loss of the original cut in tax rates. For example, assume that the marginal rates are cut enough that tax revenues are decreased by $25 billion. If the tax system collects an average of 20 percent of income, total incomes must rise by $125 billion before the lost revenue will be recovered. In the extreme case, this would require that all of the original tax cut would be saved, invested, and then generate $5 in new income for each dollar invested. It is more likely that less than half would be saved and invested and that the new income generated would be less than $5 for each $1 invested. Thus, part, but not all, of the tax cut would be recovered during the first year. That part of the tax cut not saved will, of course, be consumed, or spent on current goods and services. While this spending will also create a multiple growth in income (perhaps even to the $125 billion level) it does so by expanding demand rather than supply. An expansion in demand would be inflationary unless a corresponding increase in supply occurred. Supply-siders argue for tax cuts that will be channeled into saving rather than consumption, so funds will be made available for investment and a resulting increase in long-run supply can occur. After several years the lost tax revenue may be recovered, but only if economic growth is greater than it would have been without the tax cut because of the new investment and new incentives to produce. But once again these effects are difficult, if not impossible, to measure and assign to specific causes.

The second part of the supply-side theory is a return to a world gold standard.[4] It is argued that such a standard is required to prohibit monetary authorities from overissuing the money supply and generating inflation. Under a gold standard new money could be issued only if additional gold were available. Once the money supply was brought under control, inflation would be eliminated. A gold standard would also eliminate the ability of the federal government to use budget deficits to finance expenditures since deficits also tend to create a monetary expansion. Once monetary stability and budget balance are created, the private sector would respond to tax incentives for expanded investment, and new employment and economic growth would follow. A more complete analysis of a return to the gold standard will be delayed until chapter 7.

Monetarism

The second theoretical basis for Reaganomics comes from the Monetarist theory associated primarily with Milton Friedman, the Nobel Prize winning economist from the University of Chicago. Dr. Friedman has been one of the leading critics of Keynes and the use of an active fiscal policy. His argument has been that budget deficits and surpluses do little to determine the level of total demand, but they do have major impacts on financial markets, the money supply, and interest rates. Therefore, an active fiscal policy has its effects through the monetary sector, and then only if it affects the supply of money. Friedman's recommended stabilization policy consists of a constant, or stable, rate of growth in the money supply, set at approximately the desired rate of real growth in annual output.

Monetarist theory is the modern version of the classical quantity theory of money. In its original form the quantity theory argued that there was a direct and proportional link between the supply of money and the level of prices. That is, an increase of 10 percent in the money supply would result in a similar 10 percent increase in prices. The theory assumed that full employment existed and that each new dollar of income would be spent at the same rate as previous income. Public policy would then consist entirely of control of the supply of money. The economy was viewed as essentially self-correcting and stable in the long run. The quantity theory in one form or another provided the basis for public policy until the Depression began in 1929.

When the Great Depression destroyed the faith of policymakers in the ability of the market economy to create full employment automatically, they turned to the Keynesian alternative of active intervention through managed fiscal policy.

In the mid-1950s Friedman offered a restatement of the quantity theory that again placed control of the money supply as the primary policy weapon against unemployment and inflation.[5] Friedman argued that money was only one of a number of assets that yield services to the holder. The demand for money was expressed as a function of such variables as the price level, real income, the rate of interest, and the rate of change in prices. An increase in the supply of money would cause a change in one or more of the demand variables and increase the demand for money until demand and supply were equal at a new level. In the adjustment process the levels of income or prices would increase, or interest rates would decrease. Policymakers could thus exercise control over important financial variables through control of the supply of money.

Friedman conducted a number of important statistical tests of his theory, and in every case the results showed a very strong relationship between the supply of money and the level of output and prices.[6] While much debate and controversy followed these tests, the Monetarist influence on public policy continued to grow throughout the 1970s.

A major contention of the Monetarists is that the recent inflation has been created by excessive growth in the money supply. It follows that the recommended solution is to decrease that rate of growth. Since control of the money supply is in the hands of the Federal Reserve Board of Governors, Reaganomics requires close cooperation with Federal Reserve authorities—primarily Chairman Paul Volcker.

Prior to October 1979 monetary policy attempted to exercise control of financial markets through control (or influence) over the level and structure of interest rates. This followed from Keynesian theory that argued monetary policy has its impact indirectly through interest rates and investment. However, in October 1979 the Federal Reserve announced a major change in policy emphasis, shifting to a money supply target instead of an interest rate target. Further, the Federal Reserve began to tighten the rate of money supply growth in an effort to decrease inflationary pressure. While some critics have questioned the Federal Reserve's ability to implement this policy goal, the announced goal is in itself a major change in the direction of monetary policy.

Monetarist theory fits into the Reagan policy program because it shifts emphasis for controlling inflation from the federal budget (fiscal policy) to the monetary authorities. This shift should then leave the president free to use fiscal policy to stimulate investment and to reorder national priorities without fear of jeopardizing the battle against inflation.

Rational Expectations

The theory of rational expectations does not occupy the same relative importance as tax cuts or monetarism as a basis for Reagan's economic program, but it can be used as a basis for justifying some of the major changes in the direction and emphasis of policy. It is also used to argue that the new Reagan approach to economic policy will restore confidence and create new positive expectations for the future.

The theory of rational expectations argues that consumers and taxpayers are rational beings who use all available information to make their economic decisions.[7] Further, they come to anticipate impacts of economic policy and to react to those expected impacts. Because they anticipate policy they may actually react in ways that can counteract policy effects.

People will not make consistent errors in judgment regarding public policy. That is, having been fooled once, or even twice, they will come to anticipate policy moves and react accordingly. For example, during the 1960s and 1970s every time the unemployment rate began to rise, policymakers attempted to raise the investment tax credit (a business tax write-off for investment in new equipment and machinery). Soon businesses began to anticipate such increases and whenever unemployment started to rise, business investment fell as businesses postponed new investment until after the increase in the tax credit. The result was a fall in investment and then a large increase right after the tax credit was raised. While some observers pointed to the positive impact of the tax credit, others pointed out that the long-run investment trend was not altered. Thus, if individuals or businesses come to expect certain policy changes, they build into their decision making a course of action involving that expectation. Over time, economic policy will become less and less effective unless it surprises people by moving in an unexpected direction. Active monetary and fiscal policy becomes ineffective or even counterproductive unless it is random and inconsistent—something no policymaker would want to advocate.

Proponents of rational expectations theory would argue that the best economic policy is a long-run stable and consistent policy that can be fully anticipated by all market participants rather than an active policy of adjusting to every short-run market fluctuation that may unintentionally result in aggravating those fluctuations. A stable policy would—if people really believed it would be consistently stable—cause people to make economic decisions on the basis of independent market expectations, knowing that public policy would not create random disturbances in the marketplace.

Reaganomics has adopted rational expectations in the sense that the president's program calls for establishing a long-run policy program of reducing government involvement in the economy and the creation of monetary and fiscal stability in an effort to create a favorable climate for personal saving and business investment. The president believes that the government's role in the economy should be limited to a few selected basic programs and that the federal budget should not be used as a policy tool for short-run stabilization of incomes and prices. He further believes that monetary policy should consist of a fairly low but steady rate of growth in the nation's money supply. All of these views are consistent with the rational expectations theory.

Reaganomics places a major emphasis on the creation of positive expectations and the restoration of confidence in the private sector. The importance of confidence and rising expectations to the president's program cannot be overemphasized. The president's tax program is designed to generate increased saving and create funds for private business investment that will in turn create new employment and increased incomes. This is the expansion of the economic base that Laffer depended on to develop the arguments for expanding the supply-side of the economy. The success of the supply-side theory, and ultimately of Reaganomics, is dependent on the ability to create the necessary positive incentives and expectations. As will be shown later, the president sold his tax and spending proposals to the Congress on the basis that these expectations would be created and would in turn create a tremendous expansion in the private sector. In fact, the president's weakness may be that he oversold the ability of his program to create positive expectations and in the process created expectations for the success of the program that cannot be met.

Natural Unemployment Rate

An important extension of monetarist theory is the argument that there is a natural rate of unemployment that is determined by resources, technology, and competition, and cannot be altered in the long run by using monetary and fiscal policy.[8] Most Monetarists argue that the natural rate of unemployment is currently in the range of 5 to 6 percent, just slightly higher than the official full employment goal of 4 percent unemployment used for policy purposes during the past four decades. If this is correct, then any attempt to lower the unemployment rate through expansionary monetary and fiscal policy may lead to a short-run reduction, but will also increase inflationary pressure as the economy attempts to return to the natural unemployment rate. Furthermore, if left alone, the private economy will always return to the natural rate. So, if the short-run unemployment rate exceeds the long-run natural rate, the appropriate policy would be to stimulate private sector growth.

If one believes that monetary and fiscal policy can create only temporary changes in employment, but can have significant impacts on inflation, then the appropriate policy mix is clear. Policy will be used to fight inflation through a slower growth in the money supply, recognizing that some short-run increase in unemployment may occur. However, in the long run, economic growth and stability will increase employment until the unemployment rate returns to the natural level. Thus, when President Reagan is accused by critics of being indifferent to the problem of unemployment, it is due to his belief that there is little that public policy can do except stimulate the private sector to create more jobs.

Conclusion

All of the major theoretical bases for Reaganomics are consistent with the president's politically conservative background and his philosophy of limited government and an expanded private sector. However, the president's conservative philosophy also calls for an expanded defense budget. A large short-run expansion in defense is inconsistent with the economic program of tax cuts, limited government expenditures, and expanded private investment. An increase in defense requires larger federal revenues, obtained either through a major reordering of national priorities or by waiting until economic growth can increase revenues available to finance an expansion in all programs simultaneously. It also requires a commitment of national production resources that must decrease the resources available to the private sector for new investment and production. The issue of the defense budget is certain to continue to clash with the president's economic program of tax and spending cuts.

Although the logical roots of Reaganomics lie primarily in traditional conservative economics, the introduction of the Laffer arguments gives new importance to tax cuts as a major tool of stabilization policy. Also implicit in the theory of Reaganomics is the belief that inflation is susceptible to monetary policy action while unemployment is not. Hence, a reduction in the inflation rate that results in a short-run increase in unemployment is an acceptable short-term tradeoff. But before we examine the specifics of the president's program we must look at the historical attempts to use similar economic policies.

3 THE HISTORICAL FOUNDATIONS OF REAGANOMICS

There is very little historical precedent for the president's major economic proposals. While previous tax cuts did stimulate investment and incomes, the circumstances under which these cuts were passed differed enough to cast some doubt on their usefulness to help economists forecast accurately under current conditions. The only attempt to cut government spending substantially over a short period came at the close of World War II, and again the circumstances and the type of budget cuts were very different. Monetarist theory had not formed the basis for policy since before the Great Depression of the 1930s, although Monetarists cite the evidence of recent years as proof of the money supply/price relationship. For example, Milton Friedman and Anna Schwartz have compiled a *Monetary History of the United States, 1867-1960,* in which they argue that Monetarist theory can explain all of the major business cycle fluctuations even though it was not used to develop policy for many years. Finally, although rational expectations have never formed the basis for policy decisions, the theory can be used as a new perspective to explain historical events.

While tax cuts have occurred fairly often in recent years, most cuts have been designed to stimulate aggregate demand rather than aggregate supply. In addition, cuts have been designed to reform or change the tax by adjusting the tax base to make it more fair and equitable. Both of these moves have resulted in cuts that allocated a major portion of the benefits to low- and middle-income workers. This was a direct response to the Keynesian theory of demand management, but also a response to the general feeling that the rich paid too little tax while the middle class bore a large and disproportionate share of the total tax burden.

Tax Cuts

The first significant cut in marginal tax rates occurred in the 1922-25 period in a series of cuts under the Republican administrations of Harding and Coolidge. The primary force behind the cuts was Treasury Secretary Andrew Mellon. When the federal income tax was first imposed in 1913, it included personal exemptions of $3,000, and marginal rates that took only 1 percent of the first $20,000 of taxable income and reached a maximum of 7 percent on incomes over $500,000. During World War I rates were increased to a range of 6 to 77 percent. At the end of the war a major effort was launched by Republicans to reduce the high wartime rates.[1] Between 1922 and 1925 the marginal rate structure was decreased from a range of 4 to 73 percent to a range of 1.5 to 25 percent, and a number of changes were made in the tax base.[2]

The first cut in 1922 decreased the highest bracket rate from 73 to 58 percent, repealed the wartime excess profits tax, and instituted a preferential tax on capital gains. The arguments Secretary Mellon made for these subsequent decreases were clearly based on supply-side priorities. In 1924 Congress responded with an additional cut to a 2 to 46 percent range and also retroactively refunded 25 percent of taxes paid in 1923 and instituted a 25 percent earned income credit. Finally, in 1925 Congress further reduced rates to the 1.5 to 25 percent range.

As a result of these rate decreases, revenues decreased by 23 percent between 1922 and 1923 (from $861 million to $664 million) but then increased to $735 million in 1925 and to $1.16 billion in 1928. But perhaps more importantly, revenues increased between 1921 and 1925 in all income classes over $50,000, with increases ranging from 28 to 113 percent. At the same time, 44 percent of the taxpayers at the low end of the scale saw their tax burden fall to zero.

Do the 1920 tax cuts prove or disprove the present supply-side arguments? Certainly revenue increased after the cuts, but only after an initial decrease and a three- to four-year recovery period. By 1929 revenues were barely up to the 1921 level. Since no one can project accurately what revenues would have been without the rate changes, it is really impossible to say whether the Laffer arguments are supported or rejected by this experience. But at least one critic has observed, "At a time when only a few million Americans paid income taxes and federal spending was less than 5 percent of GNP (it was 3 percent in 1929), we are asked to believe that federal income tax cuts alone powered the growth of GNP from $70 billion in 1921 to $103 billion in 1929."[3]

More important than the total revenue impacts of the cuts, however, is the impact by income class. These results do seem to support the argument that substantial cuts in the highest marginal rates will have positive effects on incentives and will result in a net increase in tax revenues produced in these tax brackets. Those taxpayers who receive only labor incomes (wages and salaries) are unlikely to be able to alter significantly their total incomes in response to any tax changes and hence a cut in marginal rates for low- and middle-income taxpayers will likely result in net revenue losses for the Treasury. However, those in upper-income brackets who earn a substantial property income from investments seem likely to renew their efforts to increase that income when tax rates are decreased.

After the 1929 crash and the resulting fall in tax revenues, the Hoover administration again increased tax rates. Rates were further increased during World War II, reaching 94 percent by 1944. Rates were reduced slightly during the 1950s, but when John Kennedy, a democrat, was elected president in 1960 the range of tax rates still stood at 20 to 91 percent and the economy had experienced an average real rate of growth of only 1 to 2 percent a year during the previous decade.

The tax cut passed in February 1964 is commonly called the Kennedy tax cut because it was introduced by President Kennedy before his assassination in 1963, and is considered to be the major example of both a demand-side and a supply-side tax cut. While the Kennedy administration envisioned the tax cut as primarily a demand stimulus, it also had a significant impact on saving, investment, and production incentives. Originally proposed as an $11.5 billion tax cut designed to stimulate demand and get the country moving again, it contained cuts at all income levels and some major investment incentives.

The Kennedy tax bill reduced marginal tax rates from the 20 to 91 percent range down to a 14 to 70 percent range, with two-thirds of the cut effective in 1964 and one-third effective in 1965. While the average cut in rates was about a one-fourth reduction at all levels, the highest marginal rate was reduced from 91 to 70 percent. In addition, Congress decreased the corporate income tax rate from 52 to 48 percent, increased the capital gains exclusion, and made a number of structural changes in the personal income tax base. This reduction provided a large tax break for those who earn high incomes and who do a majority of the personal saving in the United States. Supply-siders argue that the extra savings and the resulting investment provide an excellent example of how to use the tax system successfully to stimulate supply.

Personal savings increased by more than 50 percent in the two years following the tax cut and capital spending rose by one-third, matching the growth of the previous decade. In part, this growth was also a result of depreciation changes and the 7 percent investment tax credit introduced in 1962, but supply-siders argue that it also reflects a climate of business confidence in the ultimate success of the Kennedy economic program.

While there is insufficient evidence to prove whether or not the creation of a $12 billion deficit due to the tax cuts ever resulted in a Laffer response and a net revenue gain, business conditions, employment, and output certainly did grow, and eventually so did tax revenues. The Treasury estimated that the 1964-65 cuts would result in net revenue losses at all income levels, but made no long-run projections concerning the ultimate impacts on total revenues. In fact, between 1963 and 1965 revenues increased in all classes over $10,000, with increases ranging from 11 to 85 percent. Total revenue declined from $48.2 billion in 1963 to $47.2 billion in 1964, but rose again to $49.5 billion in 1965 and to $62 billion in 1967 (a 31 percent increase over 1963).[4]

Do these figures support supply-side projections? Again, it is difficult to say positively. While income tax revenues increased by 31 percent between 1963 and 1967, revenues increased by a similar 31 percent between 1959 and 1963, an equal time period without a major cut in tax rates. Further, one might argue that tax changes in the form of changes in depreciation rules and the introduction of the investment tax credit were primarily responsible for the increase in saving and investment. The economic statistics for the period show only what changes occurred, not any cause and effect relationship. If one wants to believe in supply-side policy, statistics do show an increase in the relevant values. However, if one is skeptical, the increases can easily be traced to other causes or argued to be only as large as would have been expected anyway. Again, the theory for tax cuts to stimulate supply cannot be proved or disproved using available historical evidence.

One must also remember, however, that the economic conditions of the early 1960s were very different than those of the early 1980s. There was virtually no inflation in the Kennedy years, and the unemployment rate was in the 5 to 6 percent range. The federal budget was still less than $100 billion and budget deficits of $5 to $10 billion were considered normal. In the Reagan economy, the inflation rate was double digit, the unemployment rate over 7 percent, and interest rates were at an all-time high. The federal budget was in the $700 billion range, and deficits in the latter part of the 1970s had been about $60 billion. The federal government had grown from taking a one-sixth share of output in the 1960s to more than one-fifth by 1980. In addition, the tax revolt, the energy crisis, major changes in the structure of the international financial system, and major shifts over two decades in national spending priorities had all affected the role of government, as well as the ability and the desire to save and invest. President Reagan clearly did not begin his administration under the same economic conditions that President Kennedy had twenty years earlier. Nevertheless, the success of the Kennedy tax cut has provided the major historical evidence offered by supply-siders that their program will work in practice as well as in theory.

One of the first supply-siders was a congressman from New York named Jack Kemp. Kemp, a former professional football quarterback, is a conservative Republican who is generally credited with proposing the first major supply-side legislation. First elected to Congress in 1970, Kemp became converted to the value of tax cuts early, and by 1974 he introduced the first of his major tax bills, the Savings and Investment Act.[5] The bill proposed an increase in the investment tax credit from 7 to 15 percent and an increase in the asset depreciation range from 20 to 40 percent; permitted a capital gains exclusion of $1,000; and allowed a tax credit for increased saving by individuals.

By 1975 Kemp had hired Paul Craig Roberts as a staff economist and they teamed up with Dr. Norman Ture, a Washington consultant who developed a supply-side econometric model. The Ture model predicted an incredibly strong supply response to the Kemp tax bill. The following table shows Ture's analysis of the increases that would result from the Kemp tax bill.

Ture's Model — Increases from Kemp Tax Bill

	GNP	Capital Outlays	Federal Revenues	Employment
1st Year Increases	$151.4 bill.	$74.6 bill.	$ 5.2 bill.	8.7%
2d Year Increases	$200.5 bill.	$77.9 bill.	$14.6 bill.	10.6%
3d Year Increases	$248.9 bill.	$81.1 bill.	$25.2 bill.	12.4%

GNP was thus projected to rise by $600 billion over three years, or 39 percent in real terms, while employment would increase by almost 32 percent over the same period.[6] The analysis came under considerable criticism. For example, Dr. Walter Heller, chairman of the Council of Economic Advisors under Presidents Kennedy and Johnson, said that the analysis "stretches both credulity and facts."[7]

Also in 1975 Kemp met Jude Wanniski and Arthur Laffer. Wanniski was already writing editorials for the *Wall Street Journal* advocating tax cuts[8] and soon became a leading Kemp supporter. Laffer added the theoretical arguments Kemp needed to justify his tax cut proposals. Finally, in 1977 Kemp teamed up with Senator William Roth of Delaware to propose a Kennedy-style tax cut.

The Kemp-Roth tax bill was introduced in July of 1977 and quickly became established as official Republican party policy, with virtually every Republican in the House as a cosponsor. The bill proposed a reduction in rates from the 14 to 70 percent range to an 8 to 50 percent range, or a 30 percent reduction. Later versions modified the bill to spread the tax cut over three years at 10 percent each year and included tax indexing and spending limitations.

The Kemp-Roth bill was endorsed by candidate Ronald Reagan during the 1980 campaign and became the center of the election controversy. During the primary campaign George Bush (later Reagan's vice-president) called the proposal "voodoo economics," and President Carter made it a major issue in an effort to prove that Reagan would follow an unconventional and irresponsible tax policy. When Reagan was elected, the Kemp-Roth proposal became an integral part of his Economic Recovery Plan.

A slightly different approach to the supply-side tax reduction arguments came to California in 1978 in the form of the Proposition 13 property tax cut. Proposition 13 was the work of Howard Jarvis and Paul Gann and reduced California property taxes by almost 60 percent, or roughly $7 billion. The cut was accomplished by limiting the tax to 1 percent of the cash value of the property, based on the 1975 assessed value. It further limited future increases in assessments to 2 percent a year, unless the property was sold, and also prohibited future tax increases or new taxes unless approved by a two-thirds vote.

It is doubtful that Proposition 13 was conceived originally as a test of supply-side theory, but its timing provided a forum for Laffer and other supply-siders to present their theories and advocate passage of the proposition. The proposal was actually the result of many years of effort by many groups in California to enact a property tax limit. Increasing property values and automatic increases in assessments to keep the assessed values at the legal 25 percent of market value led to property taxes that were increasing at rates that often strained both household budgets and tempers.

Proposition 13 became the center of controversy in California for a year or more before it was finally approved in June of 1978 by a 2-to-1 majority. Dr. Laffer and Dr. Charles Kadlec estimated that the tax cut would result in a ten-year increase in income in California of $110 billion, would cost only $4 billion in property tax loss, and would increase other state and local tax revenues by $8 billion.[9] Other economists, however, forecast an increase in unemployment, a loss of income, and a forced reduction in public goods and services.[10]

With the passage of Proposition 13 and the expected $7 billion tax loss, local government turned to state government for relief. The state responded with a $4.3 billion bailout from the state budget surplus. The state bailout, followed by a $4.9 billion amount the following year, prevented the drastic immediate reductions in public services that opponents had predicted, but the elimination of the state surplus in 1981 brought a delayed reaction and further service reductions.

Was Proposition 13 successful as a supply-side test case? The answer again depends on what figures one wants to believe. For example, assessed property values grew 17.8 percent in 1981, and private employment in the state grew 4.6 percent, dropping California below the national average unemployment rate.[11] Property taxes fell from 62 percent above the national average (third highest in the country) to 11 percent below average (27th place). State and local government employment fell by 50,000 workers over the three-year period following Proposition 13.[12] Supply-siders would view these trends as positive results of the tax cut.

Critics point out that Proposition 13 also has had negative impacts. The cut actually resulted in a shift of the tax base from the relatively stable property tax to the more volatile sales and income taxes. As a result, the 1981-1982 recession took a severe toll on state revenues. The consequences have been significant service reductions. The state budget has gone from a pre-1978 surplus of $5.8 billion to a $2 billion 1982 deficit, bringing budget cuts for schools, public health, and highway mainte-nance. Oakland has a 200-year maintenance schedule for streets, while Los Angeles has only a slightly better 120-year schedule. The California education system, once ranked in the top six states, now ranks 44th in proportion of income devoted to educa-tion, while the pupil-teacher ratio now ranks as the highest in the nation. Many businesses also complain that the lack of ser-vices is driving new high-technology firms to other states.[13]

While Proposition 13 reduced taxes and public employment, it has also helped reduce the level of public services. Whether income, employment, and investment grew as a sole result of the tax cut is as speculative as whether they are now falling solely because of the recession.

Expenditure Cuts

The only significant cut in government spending occurred in 1945-47 when the end of World War II resulted in a decrease in defense spending and a cut in total expenditures from $95.2 bil-lion in 1945 to $36.9 billion in 1947. This cut, however, came at a time when pent-up consumer demand was more than sufficient to compensate for the government decrease and to eliminate any decline in aggregate demand for goods and services. The Federal Reserve pegged interest rates at extremely low levels in an effort to reduce borrowing costs of the Treasury, so private borrowing was inexpensive and investment opportunities and potential bus-iness expansion seemed almost unlimited. Since the United States was virtually the only industrial nation not destroyed by the war, international trade opportunities for it were limited only by customers' ability to pay, not by competition from foreign suppliers.

Government transfer payments in the 1945-47 period accounted for less than one-fifth of total spending, and government accounted for only 16 percent of the total output of goods and services. The only spending that was cut significantly was defense. By comparison, the 1980 economy was characterized by inflation, unemployment, high interest rates, a significant government sector consisting primarily of transfer payments, an already overextended private sector, intense foreign trade competition, and a general pessimism concerning the climate for business investment and expansion. In this environment President Reagan was to propose significant reductions in the federal budget, primarily social welfare programs, while vastly increasing the budget for national defense.

While the budget cuts in 1945-47 resulted in very few major adjustments for the economy, and the shift from a wartime government dominated economy to a peacetime private sector economy was unexpectedly smooth, the 1980-82 cuts have created major adjustment problems because there has been no corresponding increase in the private sector to offset government budget cuts. While the administration originally projected significant increases in private investment, the recession created by tight money and federal cutbacks has created an atmosphere of pessimism, and high interest rates have choked off any potential expansion. The resulting adverse impact of the Reagan cuts on employment and personal incomes has been very large.

Money Supply Growth

Although the October 1979 policy change of the Federal Reserve signaled a major shift toward a Monetarist theory, previous experience with such a monetary policy is surprisingly limited. Monetarists have studied in detail the correlation between changes in the money supply and subsequent changes in the level of incomes, but during most of the past four decades the policy target of the monetary authorities has been the rate of interest and not the supply of money. Since the Federal Reserve can exercise effective control over only one target at a time, concentration on interest rates tended to allow the money supply to fluctuate. Since October 1979 the emphasis on reducing the growth rate of the money supply has allowed the rate of interest to increase in response to a tight money market.

Most economists attribute the 1981-82 recession to the Federal Reserve's tight money policy, which began in 1979. Monetarists argue that the slower growth rate of the money supply was necessary to combat the inflation that had become progressively more burdensome during the 1970s. While all of the policy arguments and changes cannot be discussed here, the Federal Reserve's experiment with monetarism has not been an unqualified success, nor has it been universally popular. Nevertheless, it has been an important part of President Reagan's overall economic program.

Rational Expectations

While rational expectations have not been the basis for historical policy moves, they can be used to analyze the relative success or failure of major policy shifts. The major change that resulted from the Kennedy tax package is important because it represented an untested change in tax policy based on Keynesian demand management theories. It also occurred in a noninflationary environment and was fairly evenly divided between personal and corporate income. As a result, it stimulated both personal consumption and business investment.

In the inflationary environment of the late 1960s and 1970s taxpayers came to anticipate annual price changes and periodic attempts by government to stimulate demand through tax cuts (by adjusting the tax base rather than marginal rates) and to expand government regulation and involvement in the private economy. These expectations led taxpayers to expect less from the private sector and more from the public sector. It also helped create the atmosphere of decreased confidence in business and a belief that government policy was ineffective and national spending priorities were misguided.

While Reaganomics can find some historical basis for its policy prescriptions, the evidence from the past is neither overwhelming nor convincing. The major portions of the president's program were still largely untested when he took office in January 1981. Nevertheless, the historical precedents did exist and the evidence was strong enough that Congress was willing to experiment on a scale untried for many decades. Whether this experiment was based on conviction, hope, or simply frustration with the apparent failures of the Keynesian demand management experiments of the past two decades is a question that will probably never be answered fully—but is certain to be debated for many years.

4 THE REAGANOMICS ECONOMIC RECOVERY PROGRAM

President Reagan's economic program is a conservative response to the apparent failure of the liberal programs of the 1960s and 1970s to achieve the goals of full employment and price stability. While the liberal programs concentrated on the full employment goal, Reaganomics clearly concentrated on the goal of price stability—even at the expense of an increase in short-run unemployment. While the employment goal is not unimportant, it does occupy a secondary role in the president's hierarchy of objectives.

During the mid-1960s many economists talked of being able to use demand management tools to fine tune the economy to maintain an indefinite period of both full employment and stable prices. However, the Vietnam War and the Great Society social welfare programs shattered those dreams and introduced the longest sustained period of inflation in this century. By the 1970s the combination of high inflation rates and high unemployment rates placed Keynesian demand management policies into a dilemma that could not be solved using the traditional tools of monetary and fiscal policy. The preoccupation with cutting the unemployment rate to the arbitrary 4 percent level through expansions in government spending and aggregate demand led to new inflation pressures that the Federal Reserve then tried to reduce with higher and higher interest rates.

President Reagan was clearly elected with a mandate to solve the inflation problem. He proposed to do so without a serious increase in unemployment by implementing a program to shift the responsibility for creating jobs and economic growth from the public to the private sector.

The president's program contained four specific parts. The first, and perhaps most important to the president's overall goals, was a substantial cut in personal income tax rates. The second was a cut in nondefense expenditures, accompanied by an increase in the outlays for defense. The third was a program to reduce the regulatory burden on business, and the fourth was to encourage the Federal Reserve to maintain its Monetarist policies of slowing the rate of growth in the supply of money.

These four parts of the president's program were closely interrelated and attempted to accomplish a number of related goals. The overriding objective was to reduce both the absolute and the relative size of the federal government. The corollary to this goal was the desire to increase the size of the private sector. These goals were to be reached through the president's program to restore confidence in business and create optimism and rising expectations for the future of the private economy. The tax program was expected to increase private savings and provide funds to finance growth in private investments. Increased saving and investment would cause inflation to subside so that interest rates would fall and employment would increase. The ability of the program to accomplish all of these goals was dependent on the ability to restore business confidence and create rising expectations.

While the president's tax reduction proposal was substantial, most taxpayers would discover their total tax bills still increasing after the passage of the president's program. Tax bracket creep and scheduled Social Security tax increases would offset most or all of the income tax rate reductions for many families. However, without the president's tax reductions, total tax bills would have been correspondingly higher.

President Reagan's Economic Recovery Program was submitted to Congress in mid-February 1981 and included four basic, independent, but related parts.[1] First, he proposed a 30 percent reduction in personal income tax rates by 1984, with the first reduction of 10 percent to take effect July 1, 1981. He also proposed substantially faster tax write-offs for depreciation of new business investments. Over the three-year phase-in of the rate cuts, the 70 percent top tax rate would be reduced to 50 percent. This would stimulate personal saving and, together with the increased depreciation allowances for business, greatly expand the funds available for investment in new capital goods.

These tax cuts were estimated to reduce federal revenues in fiscal 1981 by a total of $8.9 billion. The 1982 revenue loss was expected to be $53.9 billion, increasing to $100 billion in 1983 and $221.7 billion by 1986. The tax cuts would also reduce the federal government's share of GNP from 21.4 percent in 1981 to 19.6 percent in 1986.

The second part of the president's program was proposed cuts in federal spending of $4.4 billion for fiscal 1981, $41.4 billion in 1982, $79.7 billion in 1983, and $123.8 billion by 1986. These proposed cuts would reduce the federal government's share of the nation's total output of goods and services from 23 percent in 1981 to only 19 percent by 1986. Included in the cuts were reductions in eighty-three major programs, including reductions in nearly every program except national defense and Social Security. The president promised to maintain a safety net under six programs, including Social Security and basic unemployment compensation benefits.

The president also proposed a total of $188.8 billion in national defense spending during 1981, an increase of $4.4 billion over President Carter's earlier budget. National defense was scheduled to rise to $285 billion by 1984, or 32 percent of total spending, compared with only 24 percent in 1981. These spending changes would constitute a massive shift in the direction and priorities of the federal government.

The proposed Reagan budget would produce deficits of $54.5 billion in 1981, $45 billion in 1982, and a balanced budget by 1984. By 1984, budget outlays would be $771.6 billion, compared with $654.7 billion in 1981. The rate of growth in spending would be slowed substantially while revenues would be rising rapidly in response to the tax cut incentives. The president's estimates of growth in economic variables such as inflation, unemployment, and total output clearly reflected the optimism of his supply-side advisors.

The third part of the Reagan program was a substantial reduction in regulatory interference by government over private business. Vice-president George Bush was appointed as chairman of a select committee to review government regulations and make recommendations for eliminating any regulations that unnecessarily increased business costs or reduced competition. This is the least publicized portion of the president's program, yet it is an important part of his overall plan to reduce the role of government and to increase confidence in the business sector.

The fourth part of the program involved cooperation with the monetary authorities (the Federal Reserve Board) to hold the growth rate of the money supply to a rate considered noninflationary. The official Federal Reserve target range of 2.5 to 5.5 percent per year was generally acceptable to the president. Since the president has no direct daily control over the Federal Reserve, this is the portion of his overall economic recovery plan that he was forced to place in the hands of Chairman Volcker and the Federal Reserve Board.

Few people outside the administration expected the president to be successful in obtaining congressional approval for the tax and spending portions of his program. The tax cuts were structured to stimulate saving and hence provided large tax savings to the wealthy and to business, while the spending cuts were aimed at nondefense programs. Although the Senate was controlled by the president's own Republican party, the House was still dominated by the same Democrats who had previously passed the social welfare programs, reduced defense spending, and opposed any tax cuts that were not primarily designed for relief of low- and middle-income families.

The president lobbied for passage of his program on two fronts. The first was in the Congress itself, where the president and his advisors attempted to sell their supply-side theories as the wave of the future. They also argued that the policies of the past were clearly not working and a new approach was the most likely way to achieve the results of growth and a reduction of inflation that everyone seemed to want. The second front was a direct appeal to taxpayers to support the president and let members of Congress know the will of the public. Such lobbying efforts paid off, and by early summer it was apparent that the Congress would pass both a tax cut and a spending bill that closely approximated the president's proposals.

The final tax legislation was passed July 29th and provided for an astounding revenue loss to the federal government of over $700 billion over a five-year period.[2] The final spending bill authorized budget reductions of $35.1 billion in 1982 with an additional $6 billion expected to be taken from off-budget programs.[3] The president had been successful in getting the total dollar cuts he wanted but was forced to make compromises on budget details. Most of the tax and spending cuts were scheduled to become effective October 1 at the start of fiscal 1982.

The Budget Details

The Economic Recovery Tax Act of 1981 was signed by President Reagan on August 13 and was hailed as the biggest tax cut in the nation's history. Personal income tax cuts accounted for over $550 billion over the five-year period, with business cuts accounting for another $150 billion, and estate and gift tax cuts reaching over $12 billion.[4] The major cut was an across-the-board reduction in personal tax rates by 25 percent, with 5 percent effective on October 1, 1981, and an additional 10 percent on July 1 of both 1982 and 1983. This reduction was expected to save taxpayers $494 billion through 1986. In addition, individual income taxes were scheduled to be indexed starting in 1985. Indexing is an attempt to eliminate the adverse impacts of tax bracket creep described in chapter 1. An important note on the tax rate reduction was the decrease in the highest bracket rate from 70 to 50 percent to take effect in the first year in an effort to spur private saving.

The maximum rate on long-term capital gains was reduced to 20 percent. Capital gains are gains on the sale of certain assets held longer than one year, such as real estate, stocks, and bonds. Sixty percent of these gains are excluded from the tax base, so if the remaining gain is taxed at the 50 percent maximum rate, the taxpayer must pay at most 20 percent tax on the total gain. This reduction, combined with the overall rate cut, was designed to give investors a substantial savings.

Personal saving was given two additional boosts. The first was the creation of special tax-exempt saving certificates (All-Savers Certificates), which allowed up to $1,000 interest for individuals and $2,000 for couples to be excluded from the tax base. The new insured certificates would have a one-year maturity and would be available only during a fifteen-month period between October 1, 1981, and December 3, 1982. They would be issued in denominations of $500 and pay interest at 70 percent of the prevailing rate on Treasury bills.

The second boost was an extension of Individual Retirement Accounts (IRAs) to allow $2,000 per person ($4,000 per couple) to be put into tax-exempt independent retirement accounts. The

$2,000 would not be included in the tax base during the year it was invested in the IRA and subsequent interest income would also be tax-free. It was hoped that these new incentives would encourage a large increase in the personal saving rate since they would be available to all taxpayers—even those already covered by a company pension plan.

The major tax reductions for business came in the form of a faster write-off for depreciation of investments in new plant and equipment. The new law eliminated the useful life of the asset as the standard for computing annual depreciation deductions. Instead, assets were grouped into three broad categories for depreciation purposes: three years for autos, light trucks, and special tools; five years for other equipment and machinery; and fifteen years for most buildings. These new guidelines shortened significantly the write-off periods for most assets and so greatly increased the annual depreciation deductions.

In addition to faster write-offs, the investment tax credit for equipment was increased to 10 percent and assets written off in three years would be eligible for a 6 percent credit. This credit allows a firm to take 10 percent of the cost of the asset as a tax credit in the year of purchase without affecting the depreciation value of the asset.

The most controversial new rule allowed firms with small profits (or losses) to transfer their unused credits and depreciation benefits to other firms as part of a lease agreement. This rule, known as *safe harbor leasing*, allowed companies with large profits to buy unused tax credits for cash from companies suffering losses or with profits too low to benefit from using all the investment tax credits they had available. While it helped both types of companies, critics viewed it as a way for large profitable companies to escape paying income taxes. The rule was modified in 1982 to limit safe harbor leases after July 2, 1982, and to phase them out before 1986.[5]

A special benefit for small companies was an allowance of $5,000 in 1982 (rising to $10,000 in 1986) for capital investments in the year of investment, rather than the normal depreciation allowance spread over a number of years. The ceiling for used equipment qualifying for the investment tax credit was also raised from $100,000 to $125,000 in 1982, and to $150,000 in 1985.

Finally, the corporate income tax rates were lowered for lower-income corporations. In 1982 the first $25,000 of income will be taxed at 16 percent rather than 17 percent and will be lowered further to 15 percent in 1983. The rate on profits between $25,000 and $50,000 will be reduced from 20 percent to 18 percent in 1983.

The estate and gift tax was altered to eliminate from future federal taxes all estates valued at less than $600,000, an estimated 99.7 percent of all estates. A surviving spouse will be able to avoid tax on any estate, regardless of size, while the 70 percent maximum tax rate on estates over $5 million will be gradually reduced to 50 percent in 1985.

The gift tax exemption was raised from an annual amount of $3,000 per person to $10,000 per person, and the $100,000 tax-free limit on gifts to a spouse was eliminated so any gift to a spouse would not be taxed.

The 1981 tax law also made a number of changes in tax treatment for Americans living abroad, for those selling homes, credit for childcare, and a number of other areas, including some administrative changes. However, the provisions described above are the changes the administration pushed as a basis for expanding the level of personal and business saving and increasing funds available for investment.

The expenditure package cleared Congress on July 31 and provided for a cut of $35 billion from the original 1982 budget, beginning in October 1981. Almost no programs, including Social Security old age pensions, were spared some reduction, and many programs were scheduled for substantial cuts. The exception, of course, was defense.

The largest cuts were scheduled for the food stamp program ($2.6 billion), public service jobs ($3.8 billion), and pay of federal civil service workers ($3.7 billion). Additional cuts of $1.2 billion in the nation's largest welfare program, Aid to Families With Dependent Children, $1.5 billion in Medicare, $1.5 billion in child nutrition, $900 million in Medicaid, $1.5 billion in unemployment insurance, and $1.4 billion in various Social Security benefit programs and cuts in transportation, energy, education, housing, and agriculture, left almost no program untouched by the budget ax.[6]

The 1983 Budget

The massive tax and spending cuts Congress passed for the 1982 budget were based on the administration projections showing a balanced budget by 1984, brought about by the economic growth stimulated by the supply-side policies of the 1982 and later budgets. But by September 1981 it was obvious the nation was entering a recession induced by high interest rates and tight monetary policy. The resulting fall in employment, incomes, and tax revenues and the increased pressure on the growth of expenditures for unemployment and welfare relief quickly made the budget projections (overstated to begin with) completely useless. By the winter of 1981-82, when the president began preparing his 1983 budget proposals, it was obvious that projected deficits of $100 billion or more for 1983-85 may even be too low. As a consequence, the president's new budget request called for even greater cuts in spending, but a continued commitment to the tax cuts enacted the summer before.

The 1983 budget request was for outlays of $757.6 billion and revenues of $666.1 billion, a projected deficit of $91.5 billion.[7] Private estimates placed the 1983 deficit as high as $123 billion, and the Congressional Budget Office estimated the deficit at $157 billion. These differences resulted from a wide variation in economic assumptions regarding employment, GNP, inflation, and interest rates.

The resulting budget negotiations between Congress and the president lasted for several months, during which time Reagan held firm for making further spending cuts and Congress pressed for new taxes or a postponement of the scheduled July 1 tax cut. Both were interested in reducing the budget deficit and restoring order to the budget process. Finally, in early summer the president and Congress reached a budget compromise calling for $98 billion in new taxes and a total 1983 deficit of over $100 billion. The new proposed taxes, ($21.5 billion in 1983) were primarily increases in excise taxes and changes in administration which would improve efficiency in collection rather than increase taxes owed. In return for the president's support on the tax increase, congressional leaders agreed to reduce spending $3 for each $1 in proposed new taxes. Over the three-year period, spending would thus decline by $284 billion.

Major opposition to the compromise budget came from conservative Republican supply-siders like Jack Kemp, and Democrats opposed to any tax increase during a major recession. Nevertheless, the bill passed in August 1982 and Reaganomics became the economic program responsible for both the largest tax cut in history and the largest single tax increase in history.

5 HOW WAS REAGANOMICS SUPPOSED TO WORK?

When President Reagan campaigned for office and when he presented his economic recovery package to Congress, he promised a new wave of economic prosperity, led by an upsurge in private investment spending. Despite the essentially untested nature of his proposals, he promised and expected the program to succeed in reducing inflation, interest rates, and unemployment while increasing economic growth and restoring confidence and incentives to produce. Exactly how was the president's package of cuts in taxes, spending, money supply, and government regulation supposed to work to accomplish this economic miracle?

The Tax Cut

The 25 percent cut in income taxes is an integral part of the president's program and has a number of specific goals. The first is to provide the necessary funds for an expansion in the private sector. The second is to reduce inflationary pressure by increasing the aggregate supply of goods and services relative to the demand for those goods and services. Underlying these goals is the restoration of confidence in the ability of the private sector to solve the nation's problems without interference from government.

President Reagan has argued for many years that the major economic problem facing the nation was inflation—the constant erosion of the value of money through price increases. Inflation is generally recognized as an imbalance in the market where the total demand for goods and services exceeds the supply or ability to produce goods and services. All the causes of inflation are not so generally recognized, although the prime one is an excessive growth in the supply of money. Excessive government spending and restrictions on the ability to increase supply are also believed to contribute to general inflationary pressure. Thus, while the president's primary weapon in the inflation fight was monetary restraint, a reduction in government spending and an increase in the private sector's ability to supply goods and services were important components of the total package. The contribution of the tax cut was to help expand the potential supply of goods and services.

The success of a tax *cut* as an anti-inflationary tool depends on the value of the Laffer curve to predict accurately the response to the cut. Remember that traditional Keynesian policy would require a tax *increase* as the only way to reduce inflationary pressure. The difference in the two policies is a difference in the expectation of the impact of taxes on consumption and saving.

A tax cut increases the level of after-tax income (called disposable income by economists) for a given pretax level of income. Individuals use this increase in disposable income in one of two ways—by increasing spending on consumption or by saving. A traditional Keynesian tax cut was expected to impact primarily on consumption and increase saving only by a small percentage. A Laffer tax cut would primarily increase saving and yield only minor changes in consumption.

Keynesian policy to reduce spending (aggregate demand) would thus require a tax increase, which would lead to a decrease in disposable income, and a major part of that decrease would be translated into a decrease in consumption spending, with only a minor fall in the level of saving. A tax cut would lead to an increase in consumption, which would expand the demand for goods and services and increase inflationary pressure—hence the Keynesian opposition to the idea that a tax cut is likely to be an effective policy to reduce inflationary pressure.

The Laffer (supply-side) policy would emphasize a tax cut that would be translated primarily into an increase in saving rather than consumption. If saving can be expanded significantly, new funds can be provided to the market for investment funds. If the expansion in funds causes interest rates to fall, investment projects become more profitable and attractive to business and will also increase. Investment in new plants and new equipment and machinery will increase the ability of the business sector to supply goods and services and better satisfy the existing demand.

The secret to the potential success of the supply-side tax cut depends on the structuring of the cut to insure an increase primarily in saving rather than in consumption. Economists have recognized for many years that saving is primarily a function of wealth. In fact, recent evidence shows that families with incomes under $15,000 generally have negative savings (spending exceeds income), while those families with incomes over $25,000 save enough to make the total value positive, and thus actually save more money every year than is made available to the financial markets as potential investment funds.[1]

The president and his advisors realized that if their tax cut was to succeed as an anti-inflationary tool and also provide funds for an expansion in investment, it must be structured to provide a substantial amount of funds to those who would save—the wealthy. However, proposing a tax cut for the wealthy is not politically popular, so the cut actually proposed was an across-the-board cut in rates at all levels. The average dollar cut at the lowest levels would be very small and would almost certainly be spent rather than saved. But the average dollar cut for those in the highest tax brackets would be substantial and could be expected to be saved.

This emphasis on providing funds for saving was reinforced by the impact of the tax cut on capital gains, and by the new depreciation guidelines for business, the creation of All-Savers Certificates, and the expansion of IRAs. All of these moves reduced taxes on income that was saved rather than consumed.

The second major link in the ability of the tax cut to succeed was the conversion of savings into investment in productive capital assets. Here the president's program seemed to be built primarily on the hope that business would respond positively to his program once funds from new saving were made available. In fact, the president seemed surprised and even angry when business investment did not surge immediately after passage of the tax package. There are several possible explanations for the lack of business response.

First, the economy dipped into the recession in the early fall of 1981, right before the president's program was scheduled to take effect on October 1. Few businesses will make a decision to expand investment in new productive plants and equipment at the start of a recession, especially when it is accompanied by a major shift in economic policy that will have unknown and uncertain effects. General Motors will not build a new auto plant if it already has a number of plants shut down and faces an uncertain market future. Once the recession is over and consumption spending begins to rise, business will expand if funds are available at a reasonable interest rate.

A second explanation is that interest rates remained high, with few prospects for an early decline. A truly acceptable explanation for the failure of interest rates to fall during the early part of the recession does not exist, but the uncertainty of monetary policy and the administration's budget problems is probably the best place to start.

Many people expected monetary authorities to respond to the recession by allowing an expansion in the money supply. Such an expansion, it was feared, might cause a new round of inflation or inflationary expectations. Since part of the market interest rate is believed to be an inflationary premium, a new inflationary period would bring a new round of high interest. The financial markets seem to have anticipated this possibility and have indeed built an uncertainty premium into the market interest rate.

The administration announced in the fall of 1981 that the budget deficit for coming years would be much higher than originally expected—perhaps $100 billion or more for several years. This would mean that the federal government would be in the financial market borrowing large sums of money during this period. Some estimates have placed the government share of available funds as high as one-third to one-half.[2] This, of course, would mean less money available for private investors and would push interest rates upward. Again, the market seems to have anticipated this possibility and built an uncertainty premium into the market rate of interest.

Finally, as long as the monetary authorities held to the policy of slow monetary growth, the availability of new funds from money creation would be restricted. This possibility, combined with high expected deficits and government borrowing, again would yield high interest rates. In fact, it would seem that monetary authorities would create high interest rates regardless of whether they expanded the money supply or reduced the money supply. Such was the state of apprehension and uncertainty in the financial markets as the president expected business to begin a major investment expansion.

The president also assumed that all available savings would be used for productive capital investment. Given the existing tax incentives, this assumption seems little more than a feeble hope. The wealthy did not get wealthy by acting against their own interests. Any investor is primarily interested in maximizing the real after-tax rate-of-return (the percentage rate-of-return on the amount invested after taxes). Under present tax laws a number of investments are available that tend to make investment in productive capital (plants and equipment) less attractive. For example, existing real estate and vacant land have a number of tax advantages and offer the potential for appreciation and capital gains that receive further tax preferences. Speculation in commodities, antiques, and other collectibles offers the same capital gains preferences that new plant and equipment receive, with the added advantage of possible faster appreciation in value. Thus, many savers in recent years have not put their savings in financial institutions but have gone directly to the investment market and put funds in unproductive tax shelter investments because the combination of capital appreciation and tax preference led to the expectation of higher after-tax rates-of-return. What percentage of potential funds may have been diverted from productive capital in this way in unknown, but the value has certainly been high in recent years. The impact of the recession has reduced the expected appreciation of many such investments but also created a level of uncertainty for investment in new plant and equipment.

The president's tax program was dependent on the creation of confidence and rising expectations, but they have not yet materialized. The administration's response has been to ask for more time for the program to work. The response of critics has been to pronounce the program a failure. While it may be too early to label supply-side tax policy a failure, it certainly cannot be called a success, and the longer the benefits are delayed, the greater the chance that Congress will reverse the policy and end the experiment.

The Expenditure Cut

The reduction in government spending also has two primary goals. The first was a reduction in inflationary pressure by reducing the government demand for goods and services. While the government purchase of goods and services contributes to the total level of demand, the amount of the difference between government spending and taxes (the deficit) must be financed by monetary expansion or borrowing. This expansion is then used to help finance an increase in consumption or investment demand, which increases inflationary pressure even more. The president wanted to reduce demand directly but also wanted to reduce inflationary pressure created by monetary expansion associated with government deficits. This is one reason Reagan's original budget proposal in February 1981 projected a balanced budget by 1984, created by reducing expenditures and increasing revenues from the economic growth induced by the tax cut program. Reagan has since discarded this balanced budget projection in the wake of the recession and the slower than expected reaction of revenues to the tax cut.

The second goal of the spending cuts was a reordering of national priorities from public to private spending and a reordering of public priorities from social programs to national defense. This goal is consistent with the goals of the tax cut and apparently consistent with the goals of a majority of those voting in the 1980 election. The president's intent was very clear during the campaign. He favored a reduction in transfer-type programs and an increase in defense spending. This shift has turned out to be one of the most controversial aspects of the president's entire economic program.

From an economist's viewpoint, public expenditures may be grouped into categories of (1) transfer payments, (2) payments for services, and (3) payments for goods. Transfer payments include

Social Security, welfare, and unemployment compensation, where no service is expected in return for the government payment. They are, as the name implies, simply transfers from one group or individual to another. They are the least productive government expenditure in terms of their ability to create an increase in income or new spending through additional multiplier effects.

Payments for services are primarily wages and salaries paid to government employees. While some production does take place, many of the services being provided are subject to criticism as unnecessary or as being essentially transfers, in other words, no real service is provided. As a consequence, critics of government spending argue that a reduction in federal employment may not have a serious impact on the total amount of services actually provided. However, the income multiplier is probably higher for this type of expenditure than for transfers.

The third category of public expenditures is payments for goods like defense and capital improvements on roads and government buildings. This spending yields the greatest benefit in terms of inducing additional income and employment throughout the economy. Thus, the president's reordering of government priorities should produce a long-run increase in government-induced income and employment by substituting defense spending for transfers. However, the problems created in the short run by decreasing existing programs are very real for those employed in or receiving benefits through those agencies involved. In addition, many critics believe that defense spending is a poor way to attempt to stimulate economic activity. Nevertheless, the president seems committed to his stated goals for government spending priorities. This commitment follows from his belief that the United States must regain the military superiority he believes it has lost during the past two decades. The proposed defense budget will continue to be controversial.

Control of the Money Supply

The desire to decrease the rate of growth in the nation's money supply is the one part of the president's program over which he has no direct control. Control of the money supply is under the Federal Reserve Board and its chairman, Paul Volcker. Members of the board are appointed by the president, but once confirmed they are essentially independent of both Congress and the president. Under Chairman Volcker, however, the board has followed a policy of restraint generally supported by the president.

The Federal Reserve, through its monetary control instruments, can exercise control over either the nation's money supply or the general level of interest rates but cannot do both at the same time. In addition, attempts to control the rate of interest through monetary expansion can succeed only in the short run. In the long run market forces will determine the rate of interest, with the Federal Reserve being only one force in the total marketplace. Prior to October 1979 the Federal Reserve Board concentrated on keeping interest rates low and, as a consequence, saw the supply of money increase faster than desirable for maintaining stable demand and prices. This occurred because the level of demand for funds for investment and financing government deficits exceeded available savings. The pressure was thus on interest rates to rise unless the Federal Reserve expanded the availability of new money through the nation's commercial bank lending system. A goal of keeping interest rates low is therefore inconsistent in terms of rising demand with a stable money supply. And a rapidly rising money supply tends to increase demand for goods and services, which leads to inflationary pressure and inflationary expectations.

After October 1979 the Federal Reserve Board changed its policy target from interest rates to the growth rate in the money supply. This policy required abandoning the prior interest rate policy. By not allowing an expansion of the money supply during periods of heavy borrowing, interest rates will be forced upward.

The only sources of funds for borrowing are (1) savings, (2) new money, and (3) foreign funds. Since saving was at an historically low level and the flow of international funds tended to be outward (to finance excess imports of oil, etc.) rather than inward, a slowing of the money supply rate put tremendous upward pressure on interest rates. But the slower growth of the money supply did decrease inflationary pressure, which is, of course, the reason for embarking on such a policy.

An increase in the money supply leads to an increase in the level of demand (spending for goods and services), which puts increased upward pressure on prices. Increased prices over several years tend to cause individuals to begin to expect future price increases at the same, or greater, rate. These inflationary expectations can result in higher interest rates as lenders build the loss of purchasing power into their lending expectations. The increased interest rates again cause pressure to be brought against the Federal Reserve Board to expand the money supply even further to hold interest rates down. An inflationary cycle can thus result with ever-increasing rates of monetary growth required to hold interest rates down. The only long-run solution is an eventual slowing of the monetary growth rates and an acceptance of the resulting short-run interest rate consequences.

A decrease in the rate of growth in the money supply does not have effects symmetrical to a monetary increase. A decrease leads to a fall in aggregate demand, but the short-run impact of a fall in demand is not a fall in prices but rather a fall in the level of employment and output. This is partly because markets are not perfectly competitive and because we have institutionalized price increases in the United States and made price decreases difficult. For example, indexing of wages, salaries, and Social Security benefits to increases in the Consumer Price Index (CPI) decreases public concern for inflation and pressure for solving the problem. At the same time, lack of competition means business is quick to pass price increases on to consumers, or to raise prices if demand rises, but slow to reduce prices as demand falls. The result is short-term unemployment rather than price decreases.

An increase in short-term unemployment is preferred to inflation by those who do not expect to become unemployed. Since the unemployed can obtain payments through unemployment compensation, it is argued that the adverse effects of unemployment can be minimized while the more serious problem of inflation is solved. While price increases affect everyone by decreasing the value, or purchasing power, of money, unemployment affects only a few (the unemployed and their families), but imposes on the few a much more severe burden. Prior to October 1979 the official position seemed to be that the evil of inflation was more acceptable than the evil of unemployment. Reaganomics seems to have reversed that concept and placed inflation as the primary economic evil, accepting short-run unemployment as a necessary cost of solving the inflation problem.

Outside pressure on prices, such as an oil price increase by OPEC or an excessive wage increase obtained by a major union, puts additional pressure on the Federal Reserve either to expand the money supply to help finance the additional demand or to accept even greater short-term unemployment. Again, short-term monetary growth can help reduce unemployment, but only at a cost of increased long-run inflationary pressure. The Reagan policy is clearly a preference for absorbing the necessary short-run unemployment if it means a decrease in long-term inflation.

One must also remember that the president expected the tax cut program to create a substantial increase in personal saving, which would provide the funds needed to finance business expansion even in the face of a slower monetary growth rate. If such savings did result, the impact of the monetary program on employment and interest rates would both be minimized. Unfortunately, the growth in savings has not materialized, and the expectations of large federal borrowing have kept both interest rates and unemployment at levels which threaten not only the president's economic program but the stability of the economy itself.

The Reduction in Regulation

The goal of reducing the federal government's regulation of business was obviously to reduce the cost of business so as to increase profits. During the 1970s the cost of complying with the increasing number of federal regulations imposed by an increasing number of agencies threatened to overwhelm most small businesses and imposed severe burdens on even the largest corporations.

Costs of keeping records and submitting forms for environmental protection, affirmative action, and health and safety, to name a few, increased dramatically and were essentially nonproductive. That is, they were costs that did not yield increased output and were therefore a net loss to the business. Businesses must either absorb these costs through a reduction in profits or attempt to pass the new costs on to consumers through price increases.

The president reasoned that a reduction in regulatory interference with business would lead to increased efficiency, productivity, output, and profits, while also lowering pressure for price increases. Increased output and profits could be used to create new employment and investment.

The issue of regulatory reform did not begin with the Reagan administration. Deregulation of the airline and trucking industries and passage of the Depository Institutions Deregulation and Monetary Control Act both came during the Carter administration, but both were also a response to a general feeling that government regulations often prevented the market from operating in an efficient manner.

The passage of the Deregulation and Monetary Control Act in March of 1980 was a major response to the problems of financial institutions and markets created by high interest rates, government regulation, lack of competition, and inflation during the 1970s. While not a direct part of Reaganomics, the act embodied the same principles and ideals of Reagan's regulatory reform programs. The act reduced government regulation of interest rates by eliminating interest rate ceilings and increased competition between commercial banks, savings and loan associations, credit unions, and other financial institutions. It placed greater reliance on markets as regulators, but in the process also made it likely that small, inefficient institutions would be forced out of the market.

Deregulation of airlines and trucking also created a more competitive marketplace, where marginally efficient firms found it increasingly difficult to compete and earn profits. Losses for some airlines increased and, in the case of Braniff, forced a major company out of the market. It also became possible for small regional carriers to become profitable in areas where major airlines could not justify service. Unfortunately, deregulation and increased competition came at a time when many companies were attempting to expand and carry a large debt load, and the combination of high interest rates and competition forced some companies out of the market that could have survived in less troubled times.

The reduction in regulations is the least controversial part of the president's economic program. Indeed, the only controversy is in disagreement over elimination of specific regulations. Most people, regardless of political party or economic preferences, believe government regulations had become too complicated, too numerous, and virtually impossible for the average person to even know of, let alone comply with, without a major effort. Indeed, every president in the past three decades has attempted to reorganize the federal bureaucracy or reduce the level of regulatory interference.

It may also be true that this is one area where President Reagan may have found almost immediate success. It is much easier to reduce regulatory activity in the process of budget reductions than at other times, so the president has used the budget as an effective tool for eliminating federal bureaucracy and forcing reductions in regulations where such reductions would not be feasible in times of budget expansion. Nevertheless, more reductions will undoubtedly occur in the next few years.

6 WHAT WENT WRONG?

When President Reagan signed the Economic Recovery Tax Act in August of 1981, he predicted that it would bring with it prosperity, economic growth, and a reduction in the level and influence of government in the economy. Less than a month later, published statistics indicated for the first time that the economy was moving into a new recession.[1] By mid-fall the administration began revising its previous forecasts on interest rates, unemployment, and especially on the size of the federal deficit.[2] By winter many were predicting the worst recession in the post–World War II period,[3] and by the summer of 1982 interest rates remained high, unemployment had reached its highest level since the depression, saving and investment were still at recession levels, and inflation, after a brief drop in the spring, threatened to return again to the double digit levels of past years. What went wrong with the president's hopes and expectations?

First, the recession came at the worst possible time for the president. Since his program did not take effect until October 1, only his worst critics blame it for the recession that began in August. The recession was clearly a monetary recession, caused by the tight money policies of the Federal Reserve since October 1979. These policies had created interest rates that simply could not induce investment and sustained economic growth. Businesses were finally beginning to feel the financial pinch of 20 percent interest and those that had expanded during the 1970s by borrowing heavily to finance acquisitions or new plants and equipment now could no longer tolerate the burden of such high interest rates. Some businesses failed and others began to retrench or to postpone new projects, hoping for lower interest and more favorable conditions in the near future.

The high interest rates had also taken a heavy toll on the housing and construction industries. During the last half of the 1970s real estate investment and speculation had pushed values upward at rates often exceeding 20 to 30 percent a year in some cities. By 1980, the combination of inflated prices and high interest rates priced a majority of families out of the housing market. New housing (generally financed by new loans at current interest rates) was hit hardest, and construction fell to its lowest postwar level.[4] Only the introduction of creative financing, where sellers helped finance purchases with short-term loans, kept the market active at all. But as interest rates stayed high, more and more buyers became wary of short-term arrangements that required huge lump-sum payments in two to five years.

Once the recession had started, the question seemed to be whether or not the president's program would provide the stimulus necessary for recovery. Business was obviously not as confident as the president and again postponed major new investments and laid off workers as consumer demand fell. The president's program was based on restoring confidence and positive expectations, and he clearly did not get the early response from business he expected and wanted. Instead, a year after the program began the unemployment rate had increased, investment decreased, and interest rates remained high.

By mid-fall the administration revised its projections of the federal deficit and asked Congress to approve even further budget cuts. When some members of Congress demanded a $30 billion reduction in the projected defense budget, the president responded with plans for a $13 billion cut and requested additional cuts in social welfare programs. The projected size of the 1982 deficit went from $42.5 billion to almost $100 billion, and the deficits for 1983 and 1984 were projected to exceed $100 billion. Some projections reached $150 to $160 billion in these years.[5]

By the time Reagan presented the 1983 budget message to Congress in January the deficit had become such a major issue that it threatened the president's entire budget program. During the spring of 1982 the president and Congress finally agreed on a budget that had a 1983 deficit of $104 billion, but only after further cuts in defense and other programs and the introduction of a $98 billion tax increase over a three-year period. But by summer even this compromise seemed in jeopardy when the president implied he did not feel bound by the agreement and the Congressional Budget Office projected deficits of $140 to $160 billion a year for the next three years, even with the tax increase.

The president's economic program was based on hope—hope that it would yield the results projected, and hope that it would create the confidence it required to succeed. The recession ruined these hopes and the president could then only ask for more time to let the program work. But Reagan also offered no new program to end the recession. The tax cut and a reduction in the inflation rate were assumed to be able to end the recession if given sufficient time to work. It appeared to critics that the president had only one program to cure all economic ills, and when that program failed he had no alternatives to propose.

A second problem involved the links between taxes, saving, and investment. The president assumed that a tax cut, especially for the wealthy, would bring forth a corresponding amount of saving, and that saving would in turn induce a growth of investment in new plant and equipment. Neither one of these links materialized during the first year of the program.

The tax programs designed to increase saving will undoubtedly have some positive effects, but no one outside the administration has projected the kind of response required to make the president's program successful. For example, the administration projected that the average annual increase in saving of $40 to $50 billion a year would increase to $60 billion during 1982, and to $250 billion by 1984. Even the most optimistic independent projections place the 1984 value at $90 billion, leaving a $160 billion shortfall in the administration's requirements. Saving would have to increase by more than 17 percent a year to reach the projections, and the highest levels reached during the expansion of the 1960s was only 13 percent.[6] The administration appears to have counted on an incredible combination of fortunate circumstances to realize its projections. Unfortunately few, if any, of these circumstances seem to have materialized.

One of the most publicized parts of the tax package was the attempt to stimulate savings by allowing financial institutions to offer a special All-Savers Certificate whose interest would be exempt from federal income taxes. The new certificate was a one-year savings certificate only issued between October 1, 1981, and December 31, 1982. Individuals were allowed $1,000 in exempt interest ($2,000 per couple) from these certificates.

Rather than stimulating new saving, the only real impact of the law has been to help the nation's savings and loan associations and to give upper-income individuals additional tax-free incomes. All-Savers Certificates were issued in denominations of $500 or more and paid an interest rate equal to 70 percent of the Treasury bill rate at the most recent auction. Such certificates initially paid interest in the range of 12 percent. At money market rates of about 18 percent, a couple would need to be in a marginal tax bracket of 40 percent or more to make the new certificate attractive. A couple would have to have a *taxable* income of about $40,000 a year to make the tax-free rate more attractive than an 18 percent taxable rate on other money market funds. For a couple earning only $25,000 a year, a 12 percent tax-free rate is roughly equal to only a 16 percent taxable rate, almost 2 percent lower than money market rates in the fall of 1981. Furthermore, as market rates fell so did Treasury bill rates and All-Savers rates. Low- and middle-income taxpayers never found All-Savers Certificates more attractive than taxable money market funds. Thus, the new certificates were clearly a domain of the wealthy who already had the highest saving rate.

Since there was a limit of $1,000 per person or $2,000 a couple on the exempt interest, even the wealthy could not put all of their savings into the new certificates. At 10 percent interest, a maximum of $20,000 per couple could be put into the new funds. In addition, any early withdrawal from All-Savers resulted in loss of the tax-exempt status, so the funds were unavailable for the one-year period. Current money market funds, however, were highly liquid and funds could be withdrawn in many cases on demand at no penalty. Thus, even the wealthy did not have sufficient incentive to increase greatly their overall saving rate, but rather had an incentive to move a portion of existing savings to the new tax-free status.

A second major part of the saving plan was the liberalization of IRAs so presumably everyone could (and would) respond with new tax-deferred savings programs. Savings and loan associations and other financial institutions saturated the news media in early 1982 in an effort to attract these new accounts. The total volume of new savings has increased over 1981 levels, and the ultimate impact of IRAs will probably continue to grow.[7]

In order to qualify for tax-free status, the new IRA must be kept until retirement. Early withdrawal brings substantial interest penalties and loss of the tax-free status. Thus, savers must be willing to put current income into an account and not need the money for twenty to thirty years. Most middle-income families do not want to tie up their savings for such a long period. In effect, money will be placed in an IRA only after normal savings needs are met, or if an individual does not already contribute to a retirement plan. These restrictions seem again to indicate that a majority of IRAs will be opened by wealthy rather than middle-income individuals. And since the total annual amount that an individual or couple can contribute is limited, the total volume of new savings will also be limited.

Significant increases in new savings will continue to come primarily from the increased after-tax income generated by the cut in personal income taxes and the revised depreciation guidelines for business. These measures increase after-tax income and provide the means for new savings and new consumption. But recent evidence indicates that even the wealthy are spending an unusually high proportion of their increase in disposable income. Sales of cars, jewelry, yachts, and other luxury items continued to boom while most other sales were still in the recession slump.

The president's projected link between saving and investment also appears to be much weaker than expected. While the degree to which the tax changes may have actually stimulated new investment is difficult to measure, the total level of investment in new plant and equipment has not increased. This may be, in part, a result of the recession and an accompanying decline in investment, and also partly due to the failure of interest rates to decline.[8] Business will not invest in new plants if existing plants are still idle or operating at less than full capacity.

Many critics of the president's program have pointed out that the tax cut was passed primarily on the promise that it would bring new investment and growth, and neither one has materialized. Instead, business has used a record amount of funds for financing new mergers and acquisitions, and for purchasing the company's own stock.[9] While both of these uses of funds may strengthen the companies involved, they do not produce new jobs or new goods and services. Business has apparently adopted a "wait and see" attitude toward the president's program. While surveys show a majority of business leaders still support the president and believe his program will work, their actions seem to indicate caution or pessimism about the immediate future.[10]

Because the links between taxes, saving, and investment have not been as strong as predicted, many middle-income Americans feel betrayed by the supply-side theories. They helped support a tax cut program where a majority of benefits went to the upper income groups in hopes of the promised *trickle down* benefits from investment and economic growth. Now they see the rich with even more wealth, and little evidence that trickle down theory works, especially during a recession.

The president's program stalled for several reasons. First, he clearly promised too much. Even if supply-side tax cuts work, critics argue that they could not have produced the rates of growth the president projected. In his enthusiasm to get his program passed, he promised more than he was able to deliver. Indeed, even budget director David Stockman admitted that he believed from the beginning that the president's forecasts were too optimistic.[11] The danger to the president from such false hopes is that he has lost credibility and will have much greater difficulty in the future getting Congress or the public to believe his projections or his promises. For a program based on establishing confidence, this may have been a fatal flaw in the president's strategy.

A second reason for the short-run failures was beyond Reagan's responsibility. Tight money and the resulting recession and high interest rates prevented the optimism and the growth that the president wanted. But while the creation of the recession cannot be blamed on Reaganomics, its duration and severity are the president's responsibility—a responsibility he has seemed unwilling to assume. In the midst of the worst postwar recession, the president's economic priorities have remained concentrated on inflation, the deficit, and increasing defense spending.

A third reason for the program's failure is that the supply-side links between taxes, saving, and investment do not seem to hold, at least in a recession. Tax cuts lead to increases in both consumption and saving, but the promised increase in savings from concentrating the tax cut on the wealthy has not happened. In addition, the existence of new funds does not seem to be sufficient, in itself, to stimulate new investment in productive plant and equipment.

It may be too early to pronounce Reaganomics and all of its parts as hopeless failures, but it is certainly too early to pronounce them successes. The president has asked for more time, and the November 1982 election seems to indicate that a surprising number of people are willing to grant his program some additional time. But if the program does not begin to improve soon, time will probably run out. The key to short-term improvement is certainly a continued fall in the real rate of interest, and that fall may have begun in mid-August 1982. Without continued interest rate decreases, the president's program will not succeed and will be cast aside by Congress. With continued decreases, the recession could end, investment could increase, and the president's program could be given new life.

7 WILL REAGANOMICS EVER WORK?

The answer to the question of whether or not Reaganomics will ever work is obviously a matter of "ifs." If interest rates continue to fall; if the Federal Reserve maintains or loosens its tight money policy; if Congress passes additional new taxes or postpones promised cuts; if Congress and the president reach agreement on further budget restraints; if the recession ends; and so on. Only time will tell for sure if the program works, or was even given enough time to work. But many issues can be discussed that have some bearing on the possible success of the president's plans.

Monetary Policy and Interest Rates

In early August 1982 the Federal Reserve lowered its discount rate (the interest rate on funds loaned to banks) and the prime rate began to fall. Still, Chairman Volcker maintained that the policy of tight money would be maintained but would be eased slightly. The issue of monetary policy and the resulting level of inflation and interest rates is central to any possible success for the president's program. If money stays tight and interst rates stay high, the recovery from the recession will be slow at best, and probably cannot be sustained. Yet, if the money supply begins to grow rapidly, inflationary expectations are certain to rise again and the long-term effects will be to increase both inflation and interest rates.

While the Federal Reserve faces a dilemma about the proper pursuit of monetary policy, the president's choices are more limited. He must back off of his stand on tight money and attempt to convince the Federal Reserve to expand enough to allow some decrease in short-term interest rates. A discount rate of 11 percent at the bottom of the worst recession in forty years is a difficult policy to defend when over 10 percent of the work force is unemployed. The number of people willing to accept the short-term impacts of an anti-inflationary tight money policy falls in direct proportion to the rise and duration of unemployment. Yet one reason interest rates have stayed high is the fear that the Federal Reserve would overreact to the recession, expand the money supply rapidly, and create new inflationary pressure.

This issue cannot be resolved on economic arguments alone. The political and social costs of high interest are related to the level of unemployment. If the inflation rate would show a consistent trend downward, the Federal Reserve would be in a better position to use policy to fight unemployment and the recession. But the erratic behavior of inflation through the summer of 1982 does not give a clear indication that inflation has been eliminated.

The importance of the interest rate issue as a guide for monetary policy can be seen by the fact that the Balanced Monetary Policy Act was introduced in 1982. This act would require the Federal Reserve to set interest rate targets and to report to Congress on the success achieved in reaching those targets. Introduction of this act probably influenced the Federal Reserve to loosen its money supply stance in August 1982 and allow interest rates to fall. If interest rates do not continue to fall in 1983, the act will probably be raised again.

The Deficit

The president's short-term program to reduce interest rates has concentrated on lowering the size of the federal deficit, which in turn lowers the amount the government must borrow. If government borrowing can be reduced, more of the available savings and new money will be left for private borrowing and investment. This argument assumes again that the level of investment is a function of the supply of funds. It also follows from the president's preference for private sector growth and public sector restrictions.

During the 1980 campaign Reagan consistently attacked President Carter for his inability to balance the federal budget and further argued that long-term economic stability and growth depended on a balanced budget. Yet by January 1982 the president was arguing that the size of the deficit was not important if it was created by tax cuts rather than increasing expenditures. But within a few months the president had proposed a $98 billion three-year tax increase to help reduce the rapidly escalating deficit.

The federal government is expected to borrow at least $90 billion during the last half of 1982. This is expected to help the government account for over 55 percent of all private borrowing during the year, compared to an average share of only 17 percent in the 1960s and 25 percent in the 1970s. Further, the government share is expected to remain at or above the 50 percent level for the next two to three years.[1] This level of borrowing will almost certainly crowd out of the credit markets small businesses and those private borrowers with poor credit. If so, the president's goal of stimulating investment by private business will be destroyed before it can even begin to succeed. No wonder the president's concern for reducing the deficit and the amount of government borrowing.

The extent to which the deficit can be attributed to the recession or to the president's tax reduction has been the subject of great debate. The president's defenders blame the recession and high interests rates for the failure of the tax cut to produce the promised benefits. Detractors blame the size of the 1981 tax cut, arguing that the program reduced revenues too drastically without a corresponding cut in expenditures. The president has projected revenues for 1983 to be about 19 percent of GNP, while spending is expected to remain at about 24 percent. Critics argue that a tax cut to 20 to 21 percent of GNP and a similar reduction in spending would have left the budget intact, but cutting taxes by over $100 billion in one year guaranteed budget deficits that would create chaos in the financial markets.

The president's 1982 revised budget plan was to increase primarily taxes on consumption and tighten collection and enforcement to help reduce the 1982 and 1983 deficits. If federal borrowing could be reduced without touching the income tax cuts already taken or scheduled for next year, interest rates may continue to fall and private borrowing (and investment) can then increase according to the original plan. The success of the plan also requires cooperation from the Federal Reserve to continue to loosen the money supply to help expand available funds. The risk is, of course, that the 1982 tax increase may further depress consumer spending and slow the recovery, while the deficit may not be reduced enough to allow a significant fall in interest rates. In that case, the president's plan could make the recession worse.

Reagan also suffers from an increasing lack of credibility concerning his estimate of the deficit and the size of the budget. Even when the president announced a revised estimate of the 1983 deficit of $104 billion (later $114 billion), private estimates were as high as $140 to $160 billion, and reports continue to circulate that privately the president also expects the deficit to be $150 to $200 billion a year over the next three years.[2] These reports, combined with the president's first-year admission of deliberate underestimation of the size of the deficit, give Reagan a credibility gap that increases with each new revision that increases the deficit estimate.

Two other issues are related to the deficit. The first is the attempt, assisted by the president, to approve a constitutional amendment requiring a balanced federal budget. The second is the issue of control of the so-called *entitlement* programs like Social Security and unemployment compensation. While markedly different, these two issues also address the concern over the inability of Congress to maintain control over the budget process.

The Balanced Budget Issue

The balanced budget issue is essentially a result of the view that Congress cannot, and will not, control the budget unless it is forced to do so by a constitutional restriction. At one time it was believed that a deficit was the result of recession and would be resolved by economic growth. But in the past twenty years it has become increasingly obvious that the deficit is a structural part of the congressional budget process. Congress budgets by considering each expenditure item or debt separately, then adding the sum of the parts to determine the total. Congressional budget reform in the 1970s was designed to end this process, but passing a resolution that has no legal power has not been an effective reform.

The congressional process is roughly equivalent to a household deciding how much they would like to spend on housing, then transportation, then food, etc., without considering total income available or impacts such as emergencies or loss of income. Then the amounts for each category are added to determine total spending—almost certain to exceed whatever income is available. With such a process, the existence of a recession only intensifies the problem; it does not create it. Furthermore, the passing of the recession does not eliminate the deficit. So, an increasing number of people, including economists, are arguing for a constitutional limitation on the ability to run deficits. Without such a limitation, Congress appears unable to control the budget. Critics argue that even with the limitation Congress will find a way to spend whatever it wants. For example, some additional budget items may be moved to the off-budget category where they do not appear as part of the budget. Currently such items as government guaranteed loans, and agencies such as the Export-Import Bank, Farmers Home Administration, and the Tennessee Valley Authority are off-budget. However, at the very least the amendment would be a very clear signal to Congress that a majority of people want the budget brought under control.

The balanced budget amendment was actually approved by the Senate during the late summer 1982 but later defeated by the House. By coming this close to passage, the amendment is certain to remain on the congressional agenda and be an important issue for those who feel the budget is out of control.

The Entitlement Programs

A second issue related to the budget concerns the process of bringing the budget under control through tax increases or spending cuts. The much publicized cuts in government spending have been uneven at best. For example, during the first half of 1982 spending increased by $30 billion, with six program areas that account for two-thirds of the budget rising by 21.5 percent. Spending on all other programs fell by 4 percent. Defense spending rose almost 19 percent, Social Security almost 15 percent, interest 29 percent, unemployment insurance 12 percent, Medicare 20 percent, and farm price supports 151 percent.[3]

Neither the president nor Congress has been willing to propose sufficient spending cuts to have the required impact, but both seem willing to increase taxes to make some effort at budget balancing. Unfortunately, most economists and political observers believe that a tax increase is, at best, a temporary patch rather than a permanent solution. A real budget solution will require control of federal spending—primarily the entitlement programs.

The entitlement programs represent a majority of what are often called *uncontrollable* expenditures. Entitlement programs are Social Security and railroad retirement, federal employees' retirement, unemployment compensation assistance, Medicare, and Medicaid. They are programs where citizens become entitled to receive benefits because of past taxes, health, age, prior work, or other specific circumstances. In popular usage these programs have come to mean one is morally as well as legally entitled to benefits. Congress generally establishes a benefit schedule and then the amount actually spent depends on the number of people who apply for and collect those benefits.

In addition to the entitlement programs, Congress usually considers interest on the national debt and committed outlays from prior-year contracts as all part of the uncontrollable portion of the budget. These programs collectively account for over three-fourths of the total federal budget. They are uncontrollable only in the sense that Congress does not have to vote each year to establish the benefit levels. But since Congress created the programs, they could also reduce or eliminate benefits (or the entire programs) whenever they could find the political courage to do so. Interest on the debt is the only true short-run uncontrollable item in the budget. In the long run, of course, even the national debt is the responsibility of Congress, so even interest is not really uncontrollable.

The current financial problems in Social Security acceler-
ated with the 1972 indexing of benefits to increases in the Consumer Price Index (CPI). Whenever the CPI increases by 3 percent or more, the benefits paid to Social Security recipients are
automatically increased. In the inflationary period of the 1970s
this has helped create a growth in expenditures that could not be
met even with unprecedented increases in the Social Security
tax.

When President Reagan proposed in the spring of 1981 that
some minor changes be made in Social Security benefits to help
reduce the most rapidly growing program in the budget, the
Senate immediately voted 95-0 to discard the proposal without
further consideration. The reason—an outpouring of letters,
phone calls, and public cries from Social Security recipients that
the system represented a contract between the aged and the
government that could not be broken. It could be increased, but
never decreased. Yet, it has been obvious for years that the Social
Security system is fiscally unsound and has been promising more
than it could hope to deliver. In August of 1982 Senator Dole (a
Republican from Kansas) asked President Reagan to call a special lame duck session of Congress after the 1982 elections to
solve the financial crisis in the Social Security system. While a
special session was scheduled it is unlikely that the Social Security issue could be resolved in a short period. While candidates of
both parties avoided it during the 1982 election campaigns, the
Social Security issue will require some action by the 1983
Congress.

The Social Security system is not a fully funded annuity system, like a life insurance policy where funds are built up in the
owner's name and then returned with interest upon retirement.
The system is a tax-supported annuity, transferring funds each
year from taxpayers to beneficiaries. Hence, when tax revenues
fall, or fail to increase as rapidly as expenditures, tax rates must
rise or benefits must be reduced. Congress has so far been unwill-

ing to consider the fact that promised benefits are unrealistically high, given the expected revenues. Raising taxes in the 1970s did not bring the system into balance, and new taxes probably will not bring the system into balance in the future because Congress will always promise more and more benefits.

There are four options available to the new Congress for dealing with Social Security financial problems: (1) raise payroll taxes, (2) decrease benefits, (3) transfer funds from general revenues, or (4) restructure the entire system. In 1982 the Old Age and Survivors Insurance fund began borrowing from the Disability and Health Insurance funds to make current payments because payroll taxes were inadequate to pay benefits. If such borrowing continues, all three Social Security funds will be out of money in 1984. Clearly the problem demands an immediate solution.[4]

The major tax increase proposals call for moving current scheduled tax hikes in 1985, 1986, and 1990 forward to 1984, or for forcing federal employees into the Social Security system for the first time. Both proposals would relieve the short-run cash problems but probably would not make the funds solvent for more than a few years. And since 1982 taxes can already be as high as $2,170 per worker, with the scheduled 1990 level rising to $4,075, taxpayers will certainly resist any acceleration or new taxes.

Proposals to reduce benefits take several forms. The most obvious is to alter the method used to calculate the cost-of-living adjustments made each year, or eliminate the adjustment entirely. Another option would be a gradual increasing of the retirement age from 65 to 68. This would force workers to pay taxes for three additional years and would also delay the receipt of benefits. A third option is simply to reduce current benefit levels, but such an option has little political appeal. Any choice of benefit reductions as a solution will be resisted by those receiving payments.

The third major option would be to break the tradition of financing the Social Security system exclusively through payroll taxes and transfer funds from the federal government's general budget. But since the budget is already over $100 billion in the red, transfers would keep the Social Security system solvent by having the general fund borrow even more. Such a solution can be compared to borrowing from Braniff to bail out Chrysler. It is nothing more than a shuffling of the budget.

A final option is a restructuring of the entire Social Security system. Milton Friedman has long proposed a return to the original insurance concept, paying benefits based only on the value of insurance premiums plus accrued interest. Current liabilities would be funded but future benefits would be based only on the annuity value of payments. While the system has merit as a financial alternative, it has little political expectation of passage since it leaves open the potential for millions of underfunded, starving elderly citizens.

A similar, but politically more acceptable, restructuring has recently been proposed by economists Michael Boskin, John Shoven, and Laurence Kotlikoff.[5] Their proposal separates the insurance and annuity aspects from the welfare portion of Social Security benefits. Every family would continue to receive insurance and annuity benefits according to the value of their contributions plus interest. A separate welfare component would also be calculated that would be provided to poorer families. The welfare component would be gradually reduced, and would be eventually phased out for all but the poorest families. All workers, government and private, would be included in the restructured system.

Whatever the eventual choice Congress makes, the Social Security issue typifies the problem of the entitlement programs. Such uncontrollable programs have become an excuse for political reluctance to make difficult decisions regarding the allocation of limited government resources. The fact remains that a tax increase alone is not a budget solution—with or without a balanced budget amendment. Only when Congress has the ability and willingness to budget by bringing expenditures under control will there finally be a long-run solution.

To illustrate this point, consider the August 1982 attempts by the administration to convince Congress to increase taxes by $98 billion over three years. The Office of Management and Budget argued that Congress had agreed to reduce spending by $284 billion over this period as a trade-off for presidential support for the tax increase. But the promised $284 billion cut consisted primarily of mythical cuts from previous projections of what spending would have been under those projections. In actuality, the budget was still expected to grow by over 21 percent during the three-year period to a total of $881 billion.[6] Further cuts would come from revising economic forecasts of variables such as interest rates to reflect a more favorable economic climate in the future. Such budget dealings hardly represent sincere attempts to bring spending under control, but they do allow members of Congress to argue that they are concerned budget cutters.

The Tax Issue

The tax issue also has several parts. The first is the issue over the value of the president's income tax cuts as an economic stimulus. A second is the issue of the 1982 tax increase on consumption. A third is the issue of tax reform and the proposed *flat-rate* tax.

The president and his advisors have held fast to their belief that more time is all that is needed to prove the success of the idea that income tax cuts can, and will, stimulate saving, and in turn investment and economic growth. Regardless of the arguments that high interest rates and the recession are responsible for the lack of first-year response to the tax stimulus, the theory remains unproved and the number of skeptics grows daily.

Part of the issue revolved around the arguments that the average taxpayer really did not receive a tax cut in either the first or second phase of the program. Since the cut was granted in three stages, with only 5 percent effective immediately and another 10 percent effective in July 1982, proponents argue that no substantial reductions were scheduled in the first year, so little response could be expected. Increases in Social Security taxes, as well as state and local taxes on incomes, sales, and property, are believed to have wiped out most or all of the federal income tax cut for all but the wealthiest taxpayers. Furthermore, inflation-induced increases in personal income continued to boost many taxpayers into higher tax brackets where, even after a reduction, rates were still higher than those paid before the tax cut bill was passed.

In making the argument that taxes were not really cut by the 1981 bill one researcher has argued, "Supply-side economics has not worked and will not work for one simple reason: It has never been and is not likely to be tried. Contrary to all the Congressional hullabaloo over the Reagan tax-cut package, personal tax rates will...continue their upward trek."[7]

The point that taxes were not really cut will be made often by those who favor supply-side policies. While the point is technically valid and can be used to show why there was a weak response to the president's program, it is also true that taxes were decreased significantly over what would have been paid without the program. It is not likely that supply-side tax theory will receive additional support in the near future based on the argument that the president's tax cut was not large enough to provide a true test.

The second issue concerns the desirability of raising taxes through a new series of increases designed to raise $98.3 billion over three years ($18 billion in 1983, $37.7 billion in 1984, and

$42.7 billion in 1985). The 1982 tax bill was passed by both houses of Congress on August 19 and effectively repeals one-fourth of the tax benefits granted in 1981. Part of the increase ($26 billion) is expected to come from increased policing and withholding on dividends. New or increased taxes will be levied on smokers, phone users, travelers, and those who barter. Deductions will be limited or reduced on medical expenses, casualty losses, and retirement plans, while some business benefits passed in 1981 like safe harbor leasing and depreciation will be scaled back. New taxes each year would be spread roughly equally between individuals and businesses.[8]

The president's arguments for the tax increase were discussed earlier—primarily a need to reduce the deficit and government borrowing. Opponents came from two directions. The first were hard-line supply-siders who felt that a tax increase would further decrease the ability of the prior income tax cut to prove effective. The second opponents were those who saw a tax increase in a deep recession as counterproductive to the goal of stimulating consumer spending. They also saw this particular tax increase as a further shift of the tax burden on the poor and middle classes, and away from the wealthy, arguing that the president was balancing the budget on the backs of the poor. These critics felt that a more acceptable solution would be to defer the third phase of the tax cut passed in 1981 and further increase taxes on the wealthy and on business.

Obviously the two opposing groups agreed only that the tax increase should be defeated. One group wanted more time for the stimulus on investment to work, and the other wanted either a reduction in taxes on consumption or an increase in taxes on investment. This issue could not be resolved satisfactorily with the passage or defeat of the tax bill. From an economist's viewpoint, a tax increase in the depths of the recession seemed an unlikely and unacceptable antirecession policy. But without budget control, interest rates were certain to continue to contain a risk/fear premium and remain high. In such a case the recovery was also certain to be weak and short.

The third issue is the proposal for a flat-rate tax. This proposal takes many forms, but basically calls for eliminating most existing income tax exemptions and deductions and then using a flat rate of 10 to 20 percent on the resulting comprehensive income tax base as a substitute for the present tax system. In recent years the income tax has taken about 19 percent of taxable income (after exemptions and deductions) and about 15 percent of adjusted gross income. Thus, in order to maintain the current level of revenues, a flat rate of 15 to 19 percent is required, depending on the exact definition of income to be taxed. Some proposals include some graduation of rates in three or four brackets, and almost all proposals include a standard deduction and some level of personal exemptions.

Almost no one argues in favor of the present system (except for retention of individual preferences by the vested interest groups involved), but there is little agreement on the ideal system. A flat rate would greatly simplify the tax system but would eliminate thousands of jobs for those who now prepare tax returns. In general, a flat-rate system is preferred by those now paying more than the expected 15 to 19 percent and opposed by those currently paying less. It would increase the percentage paid by the poor and reduce the percentage paid by the wealthy, with the dividing line being just under $30,000. But for many individual taxpayers who now use tax preferences to eliminate their tax completely, the new tax would be a significant increase.[9]

A flat rate without a corresponding broadening of the base would clearly be unacceptable to a majority. Existing inequities would be compounded, not eliminated. Yet the greatest obstacle to passing the new tax will be arguments by vested interest groups that their preferences are essential. If preferences are retained, the logic for the flat-rate system is destroyed.

Economists have argued for over twenty years that the tax system could be improved by broadening the tax base and lowering the tax rates.[10] The preference for a flat rate or a reduced number of graduated rates (for example, 4 to 24 percent in three or four brackets) involves a value judgment, but any graduation in rates would eliminate one of the best arguments in favor of a new system—simplicity. In addition, since most current proposals have a provision for protecting the poor by generous exemptions or zero-bracket amounts, they may be somewhat progressive even with a flat rate.

The Stockman Interview

In the December 1981 issue of the *Atlantic Monthly* magazine, David Stockman, the Director of the Office of Management and Budget (OMB), was the subject of a lengthy article and interview.[11] The article created a storm of controversy about the president's economic program because Stockman revealed some insights into how the program had been put together and pushed through Congress. It also revealed that both Stockman and the president knew that the projections sent to Congress to support the bill were inaccurate and overly optimistic. This article, more than anything else, created the credibility problem for the president's future projections.

While it is unfair to Mr. Stockman to quote from the article out of context, this is precisely what happened. For example, statements such as "I've never believed that just cutting taxes alone will cause output and employment to expand" and "Kemp-Roth was always a Trojan horse to bring down the top rates"[12] gave the impression that Stockman was never a supply-side believer but were inaccurate reflections of the ideas in the article. Nevertheless, they did cause a controversy and gave the opposition ammunition to use against the president's program.

This article needs to be read completely to get the appropriate insights into the president's budget-making philosophy. However, a few revelations need to be pointed out here. First, when Stockman arrived at the OMB in January 1981 he used the OMB computers to estimate the economic impacts of the president's program. The results shocked even Stockman, predicting deficits of $82 billion in 1982 and $116 billion in 1984. The solution—reprogram the computers with more favorable projections of inflation, interest rates, economic growth, and investment. In effect, assume the most optimistic outcome possible for the tax cut and then project it as a reality. The result was a projected deficit of $42.5 billion in 1982 and a balanced budget by 1984. This is not fraud if one really believes in the projections, but critics found it very misleading at best.[13]

The second revelation was that within the first two months after the program had been submitted to Congress, the president and his advisors knew their plan was inaccurate in its projections, promising far more than they could expect to deliver. Yet the president continued to appeal to the public for support, promising a new era of budget control when he knew a budget solution had still not been found.[14]

The third revelation was that Congress was far too willing to accept OMB projections without question, even when the Congressional Budget Office figures showed an opposite budget impact. This is illustrated by the episode of the "magic asterisk." When the OMB could not produce precise figures for reducing the 1984 deficit below $70 billion, Stockman inserted an asterisk denoting future budget reductions (unspecified) that would take care of all deficit problems. Congress accepted the asterisk and passed the program. Congress was so used to sloppy budgeting that they allowed the OMB the same privilege.[15]

The Stockman interview contains many insights into the budgeting process during the first months of the Reagan administration. Unfortunately, they are not all positive, but they do help explain why the general public, and especially the financial markets, have become skeptical of any budget projections emanating from either the OMB or Congress.

The Defense Issue

The only major expenditure category projected to increase substantially over the long run in the president's budget is national defense. The president originally requested an increase in the defense budget of 17.5 percent per year from 1981 to 1987, a growth in real (inflation-adjusted) terms of over 10 percent a year. Spending would be $183 billion in 1982, $247 billion in 1984, and $355 billion in 1987.[16]

Defense is one area on which President Reagan has steadfastly refused to negotiate. In the fall of 1981 when Stockman attempted to persuade the president to reduce defense projections by $30 billion, he got only $13 billion. When some members of Congress demanded cuts in defense to match cuts in social welfare programs, the president refused. He believes that defense has been a neglected area for too long and only an increase in these expenditures will restore America to its rightful position as the free world leader.

Critics have argued that the president seems to be taking the same approach to the problem of defense that the Democrats took in the 1960s and 1970s with social problems—if a problem exists, throw money at it until it goes away. And just as the social welfare programs of the earlier period were not solved by huge new programs and outlays, it is unlikely that the defense issue can be resolved by huge new expenditures on military hardware and personnel. In fact, even the military seems to be embarrassed by the new outpouring of funds.[17]

The president seems to be arguing that budget reductions in all other areas will reduce waste and inefficiency, but no such waste and inefficiency exists in defense. Instead, defense must be expanded as rapidly as possible, regardless of the issues of efficiency or cost. This attitude reflects the president's background and his reputation as a military hawk, but it also creates a number of problems for his budget program.

It is unlikely Congress will continue to increase appropriations for defense at a rapid rate while cutting other programs severely. At some point the president will be forced to compromise or lose the cooperation of Congress in reducing other programs.

It is also unlikely that the president will be able to reduce substantially the size of the deficit through a tax increase and cuts in social programs if he continues to demand such a large expansion in the defense budget. Regardless of his political preferences, it seems obvious that the president must reduce his budget requests for defense or risk failure of his entire budget program.

The New Federalism

In January 1982, the president announced a new budget program designed to alter the revenue and spending mix between the states and the federal government. The program, called the *New Federalism*, was not given serious consideration by Congress during 1982 but remains a part of the president's overall program to shrink the size of the federal government and shift responsibilities to states and the private sector.

The major part of the New Federalism involves a proposed swap wherein the states would take over the two largest income-maintenance programs of food stamps and Aid to Families with Dependent Children, while the federal government would assume all costs of Medicaid. The administration estimated that if the swap was initiated in fiscal 1984, the states would pick up $16.5 billion in new costs but would lose $19 billion in Medicaid expenses. Further, the savings would rise over time, reaching $7.5 billion by 1987.[18]

In addition to the program swap, the federal government would establish a trust fund using federal taxes on tobacco, alcohol, and telephones and half of the taxes on motor fuels and windfall oil profits, as well as allow states to choose between unrestricted cash grants or participation in forty-three current federal grant programs. The federal programs would be phased out entirely by 1991 and states would then be forced either to increase their own excise taxes or to eliminate programs.

The major fear expressed by critics of the program swap is that AFDC and food stamps would either become expendable programs by states pressed for funds or would be underfunded to the point of creating great hardship for those participating in the programs. States would certainly vary greatly in their willingness and ability to fund these major welfare programs, but those states without oil production would have the greatest difficulty picking up revenues lost by the expired windfall profits tax.

Critics have also argued that the administration underestimated the increased costs to the states, and in reality the states would lose as much as $86 billion a year by 1991.[19] Projections of program costs over the next ten years are obviously imprecise and subject to numerous assumptions about the future of revenues and programs, but most state officials are skeptical enough of the swap to be slow in embracing the president's figures. In any case, the program is certain to cause state taxes to rise over time, and while federal taxes are projected to decline at the same time, Congress is likely to find ways to avoid that possibility.

An added dimension to the program will come if the states ever do ratify a constitutional amendment requiring a balanced federal budget. Total federal aid to state and local governments exceeded $86 billion in 1982, up from $22 billion in 1970 and $47 billion in 1975.[20] Congress may decide to balance the federal budget by eliminating aid to state and local governments, and then letting them raise their own sales, income, or property taxes. In such a case, state and local governments would face fiscal disaster, since many are already retrenching from the effects of the tax revolt and the 1981-82 recession.

The Gold Standard

Not long after the passage of the Economic Recovery Tax Act in the summer of 1981, Arthur Laffer argued that "Gold has always been the most important issue in my mind."[21] Why should a gold standard be more important than the tax cut, which was thought by many to be the central part of supply-side stabilization policy? The truth is that hard-line supply-siders have always believed that the tax cut was only a beginning (although an important beginning) to help pave the way for the real issue—a return to a world gold standard.

The issue of a gold standard is not currently an official part of the Reagan economic program. However, the president has been a long-time supporter of the idea, and during the campaign of 1980 publicly argued in favor of a return to a gold standard as an important part of a long-run economic stabilization program. In early 1981 the president asked Congress to establish a special gold commission to be given a charge of investigating the desirability and feasibility of returning the country to some type of monetary gold standard. In early 1982 the president quietly accepted the commission's recommendation that the country not attempt a return to the gold standard. But the issue remains, if for no other reason than it provides hard-line supply-siders with an explanation for the failures of the tax cut to produce the promised benefits.

The United States and most of the rest of the free world were on some form of gold standard or bimetallic standard from 1792 until the mid-1930s. Since then we have had a domestic inconvertible paper standard, meaning that our money has not been convertible, or redeemable, into gold, silver, or other precious metals. Advocates of a return to gold argue that during the period of the gold standard the nation had long-run stable prices, and has had constant inflation under the paper standard. Thus, a return to gold would bring a return to price stability.

The issue of a return to a gold standard is important enough to require a brief explanation and analysis. Under a gold standard the price of gold is fixed by the federal government by agreement to buy or sell all gold offered or requested at the fixed price. Between 1935 and 1971 the fixed price was $35 an ounce, even though during this period American citizens could not legally own gold. In earlier years the price was $20.67 an ounce. This meant that the Treasury would buy or sell at that price regardless of the quantity demanded or offered.

The appeal of the gold standard involves the discipline over the money supply (and hence inflation) that such a standard supposedly brings. Theoretically, a gold standard will eliminate inflation since any overissue of the paper money supply that results in price increases will cause citizens to redeem their paper dollars at the Treasury for gold. As the gold supply at the Treasury falls, the ability to issue currency backed by gold will also fall, leading to a reduction in the supply of money and the rate of inflation.

A major side benefit to supply-siders of such a monetary system is the expected discipline it would impose on the federal budget. A budget deficit would lead to increased borrowing by the Treasury and an increase in the money supply as the Federal Reserve or banks purchased the new securities and used them to expand lending activities. This increase in the money supply would cause inflation and a loss of Treasury gold. Over time the Treasury would either need to stop borrowing or lose its entire gold supply. Advocates argue that deficits would vanish, inflation would vanish, and with them interest rates would return to historically low levels. Low interest rates would stimulate new investment, and the intent of the tax cut would finally be realized.

In support of the theory, gold advocates point out that the average level of prices in 1933 was about the same as it was in the early 1800s. That is, periods of inflation had been offset by periods of deflation so that prices on the average had not changed for over 100 years. Advocates often point to this price stability as a major argument for a return to gold.[22]

What the long-run averages do not indicate clearly is the fact that prices under the gold standard were never stable. The only price that was stable was the dollar price of gold. All other prices fluctuated over a wide range. In fact, prices increased by 125 percent between 1897 and 1920, but then fell by 102 percent by 1933.[23] Earlier periods saw similar kinds of price movements. Long-run average price stability does not necessarily mean short-run price stability. In addition, it is less likely that modern prices are as flexible downward as they were in earlier periods. A decrease in the gold supply and the supply of money may result in an increase in unemployment rather than falling prices. If so, stability could be maintained only if prices were prevented from moving either upward or downward.

Advocates also point out that the long-run average increase in the quantity of gold is only 1 to 2 percent a year.[24] Since the quantity available will influence the supply of money, a steady, slow rate of growth in the gold supply is desirable. Therefore, at 1 to 2 percent a year the economy would not suffer from inflationary or deflationary shocks created by wide swings in the quantity of gold available. Again, long-run averages do not indicate short-run stability. The quantity of gold may increase dramatically for a few years and then not increase at all for some time. Under a gold standard, market prices and output would also fluctuate with changes in the gold quantity.

An even greater modern concern over using a gold standard is the fact that most of the new gold sold each year comes from either South Africa or the Soviet Union. The possibility exists that the USSR could sell a large quantity of gold and create monetary instability for the United States. Another possibility is a large gold sale or purchase by Arab oil countries that could create major fluctuations for the rest of the world.

The possibility of a fixed supply of gold over a long period of time is as much of a problem as is an unstable supply. Economic growth requires an expanding money supply over time. Under a gold standard the ability to finance economic growth may be choked off if new gold is not brought into the system. A long-run rate of growth in gold of 1 to 2 percent a year does nothing for a company or industry trying to grow in the short run. A possible result of a fixed supply of gold would be unemployment, slow growth, and recession. It is clear that a gold standard would not bring stability unless the available monetary gold supply increased at precisely the rate of real economic growth. In any other case the nation would suffer from inflation or depression, perhaps even greater fluctuations than we have had under the existing managed paper standard. To work correctly, the gold standard requires that the rest of the economy be forced to adjust to the fixed price of gold. If it cannot, or will not, adjust, inflation and recession will result just as under any alternative form of monetary standard.

Perhaps the greatest obstacle to a return to gold is the issue of setting the correct price. If the initial price were set too high, or later became too high (in the sense that it was not at a market equilibrium clearing price), current holders of gold would want to sell their gold to the Treasury. This would cause an increase in the money supply and renewed inflation. If the initial price were set too low, or later became too low, gold would flow out of the Treasury, creating a money supply reduction, deflation, and recession.

Some experts have estimated that a full gold standard would require a market price of $3,000 to $4,000 an ounce,[25] while others have suggested a price of $350 to $650 an ounce.[26] No one argues that the current free market price is likely to be a good long-run equilibrium price. In the past three years gold has fluctuated between $350 and $800 an ounce, but the current market conditions under which gold is traded are so different from conditions that would prevail under a monetary gold standard that price comparisons are almost meaningless. But since there is no good way of determining the correct price, any return to gold would certainly be accompanied by a period of alternating inflation and recession as we hunted for that correct price. And if an arbitrary price was chosen and not changed, the nation could suffer severe long-run problems of either inflation or depression.

The truth is that the countries of the world went off the gold standard because it didn't work; they are likely to stay off for the same reason. Political authorities are not likely to remain idle and watch a depression worsen when discretionary policy tools are available to help correct and turn it around. While the paper standard has an inflationary bias, the gold standard has a distinct deflationary/recession bias. Gold works well in times of prosperity, but once a downturn begins, the gold standard is likely to compound the decline.

The gold standard does not work for another very practical reason—people turn in their paper money for gold during times of recession or depression, or in times of extreme inflation, but not during times of mild inflation. This means that during a recession the money supply is likely to fall, but discretionary policy in a recession would be to expand the money supply. Thus, the gold standard takes away a major tool for stabilization.

Virtually all economists agree that a managed paper standard is preferred to a fixed rate metallic standard. But most would also agree that monetary authorities in the past have had a poor record of monetary management. This has been due in part to the pressure for monetary expansion created by federal budget deficits. An end to the deficits would allow monetary authorities more freedom for monetary management.

8 STAY THE COURSE?

When Ronald Reagan took office in January 1981 he inherited a startling array of economic problems and an economic policy program that had lost its sense of direction. Stabilization policies of the past twenty years had produced confusion in the financial markets and had failed miserably in solving the two major problems of inflation and unemployment. Keynesian demand management policies failed because they were not used properly and because they had been asked to accomplish far more than they could reasonably be expected to accomplish.

Previous presidents and Congress had used demand management theory to justify an expansion of government programs and spending that had become a bigger threat to economic growth and stability than the economy had experienced since the Great Depression of the 1930s. The government budget was used to expand demand and output but was never used to contract. The arbitrary full employment unemployment rate of 4 percent was used to justify a constantly expanding public sector, while inflation and high interest rates continually eroded the ability of the private sector to provide desired goods and services.

Public policy had developed a type of ratchet effect where increased spending led to more inflation and higher interest rates, which in turn led to slower growth and more unemployment, which prompted even more government spending. These policies had produced a state of economic confusion and uncertainty by 1980 that led voters to reject them and turn to something new and supposedly different. The Carter administration had proved completely incapable of solving economic problems using the accepted policies of the past two decades. Reagan offered a new (basically untried and untested) approach to solving economic problems.

Reagan inherited an economy that had a high and rising unemployment rate, one of the highest rates of inflation in the postwar period, the highest interest rates in the nation's history, falling productivity and economic growth, the largest budget deficits in history, financial markets in a state of confusion, a rapidly expanding public sector, and a general state of uncertainty and lack of confidence in the ability of government to keep its own house in order, let alone solve the nation's economic problems.

Into this environment President Reagan proposed a four-part economic recovery program that was designed to implement a long-run recovery without attempting to deal with each separate short-run problem. The program involved (1) a massive reduction in income taxes over three years, (2) a similar reduction in government spending, (3) a reduction in the interference with business by regulation from the public sector, and (4) cooperation with the Federal Reserve in slowing the rate of growth in the nation's money supply.

This four-part program was designed to reduce the relative size of government and expand the ability and the incentives for the private sector to grow. The president believed strongly in the ability of the market economy to solve its own economic problems if given adequate time and incentive.

The logic of the Reagan program came primarily from a group of economists who proposed a theory known as supply-side management. The central part of the theory was the argument that the private sector could be stimulated by a tax cut designed to increase saving and provide new funds for business investment in new capital goods. This new investment would expand the ability of the market to supply goods and services and thus reduce both inflationary pressure and unemployment. If structured properly, the tax cut could stimulate such growth and new incomes that tax revenues would actually rise and no budget deficit need occur.

The reductions in spending, regulation, and monetary growth were designed to reduce aggregate demand and relieve inflationary pressure while restoring confidence and positive expectations in the private sector. The Reagan program counted heavily on increased confidence and optimism. Without it, and without the new investment it was designed to create, the Reagan program would produce only greater deficits, more unemployment, and more uncertainty.

If the president's program had its theoretical roots in untested water, its policy foundations were even more uncertain. Only during two other periods in United States history had massive tax cuts been passed, and in both cases the results promised by supply-side theory were uncertain. In the 1920s a series of tax cuts helped to produce an expanding economy that was cut short by the Depression. In 1964 the Kennedy tax cut increased aggregate demand as well as supply and was part of the longest period of prosperity in the nation's history. But in both cases the impact and importance of the tax cut in producing the expansions were subject to considerable debate.

The Reagan tax cut was supposed to have its impact through the creation of incentives to save and invest in the private sector. Since the wealthy do a majority of the saving and investing, the tax cut concentrated benefits at the high end of the tax schedule. The maximum marginal tax rate was reduced from 70 to 50 percent, while other provisions reduced taxes on long-term capital gains, expanded depreciation allowances, and gave corporations a number of special tax cuts. It was expected that new savings generated by these tax cuts would be used by business to expand investment in new plant and equipment.

President Reagan succeeded in pushing both of his budget programs through Congress during the summer of 1981, cutting both taxes and government spending by unprecedented amounts. Unfortunately, the tight money policy of the Federal Reserve also helped produce a recession that began in the early fall. The recession caused government spending to rise and revenues to fall greatly, expanding the predicted budget deficit and creating an atmosphere of uncertainty, primarily in the newly deregulated and competitive financial markets. In addition, the size of federal borrowing to finance deficits threatened to absorb most, if not all, of the increase in savings. As a result, interest rates remained high, and the promised expansion in business investment did not come.

By the spring of 1982, the president became convinced that only a reduction in the size of the projected federal deficit would restore confidence to the financial markets and lower interest rates. The president agreed to a $98.3 billion three-year tax increase in return for a congressional promise to reduce spending by $284 billion during the same period. Even then the administration projected a deficit of over $100 billion for several years, and the Congressional Budget Office projected deficits of over $150 billion a year.

The passage of the tax bill in August 1982 helped spur a reduction in interest rates that created one of the largest stock market surges in history. But many analysts still predicted high interest rates throughout 1982 and 1983, largely because of the belief that the federal budget was still not under control and that the Federal Reserve would again tighten the growth in the money supply to dampen any expectations of a renewed inflationary cycle.

By the fall of 1982 it was clear that the president's program had not produced all of the promised results. Unemployment was over 10 percent, the highest level since the Depression. Inflation was declining, but with occasional bursts that left doubt as to whether or not a long-run trend had really been created. Interest rates were falling, but long-term commitments by the financial sector and fear of the future course of public policy created uncertainty mingled with general optimism.

While the president's program has failed to produce the promised short-run benefits, an important issue is the ability to produce the long-run stability and growth it also promised. The president was clearly too optimistic in his enthusiasm for the benefits of his supply-side programs. But the program could not have produced all of the president's promised benefits in the first year. Supply-side policies were never intended to be able to produce a stable economy in such a short period. The economy of 1980 had taken almost twenty years to create. It is unreasonable to expect a complete change in one year. Yet the president's program is perceived by many to have made the major problems worse rather than better. Thus, an important question might be, What would the economy have been like without Reaganomics?

First, the recession would have occurred with or without a change in the direction of policy. Tight money policy of the Federal Reserve, combined with inflationary expectations and resulting high interest rates, had already put the recession forces in motion. The difference, of course, would have been the reaction of the Carter administration to the recession as it developed during 1981 and 1982. That policy would probably have been a massive expansion in public spending and a tax cut of approximately $25 to $40 billion. Both responses would have generated an expanding deficit (Carter's last deficit was $60 billion) and created a renewal of inflationary expectations and even higher interest rates. The short-run unemployment would probably have been less than the 10.4 percent Reagan rate, but the private sector would still have had no incentive to expand. In short, the economy would probably have had a slightly lower unemployment rate, a higher inflation rate, even higher interest rates, and no prospect of a viable long-run solution.

It is clear that a majority of Americans wanted a change in public policy by the fall of 1980. Ronald Reagan provided an alternative based on private market growth rather than by public sector growth. But the program offered long-run solutions rather than short-run responses. And in his enthusiasm to see his policies accepted, the president promised short-run benefits that the program was not designed to deliver. In the process, he created a credibility gap and appeared at times to be indifferent to the plight of the unemployed. Without a restoration of the confidence he originally sought, the president's program cannot succeed, even in the long run. Unless short-run problems can also be solved, the long-run may be too far away.

Several issues are central to the eventual success of Reaganomics and the ability of the program to provide long-run solutions to economic problems. The issue of the federal deficit and its impact on interest rates is crucial. But most observers believe that ultimate control of the budget lies in control of expenditures rather than further tax increases. Congress must somehow come to grips with the uncontrollable parts of the budget, such as Social Security and federal grants. If Congress does not more readily accept its constitutional authority and responsibility to budget public funds, it is likely that an amendment requiring a balanced budget will be passed and ratified by the states. Congress will also be required to create a tax system that is perceived to be more equitable and less susceptible to influence by vested interest groups.

The president is also likely to face increasingly difficult times over his determination to increase the defense budget while reducing so drastically budgets for social services. Without some new compromise on defense the president will certainly weaken his ability to push other budget changes.

An important issue will continue to be the credibility of budget projections made by the president's Office of Management and Budget. The president's original budget projections were made using the most optimistic estimates of growth and the most favorable response possible to the tax cut program. Even when the president became convinced that these projections were totally inaccurate he continued to press the case for the program, promising far more than he knew his program could be expected to deliver. Constant budget revisions, each one projecting a larger deficit and requiring more spending cuts or more revenue increases have eroded the public's confidence in the president's estimates. The only thing that is totally clear is that the budget is out of control.

The final, and probably most critical, issue is that of unemployment. By the time of the November 1982 elections, over 11 million Americans were unemployed. The 10.4 percent unemployment rate was the highest since the Depression, and 3 percentage points higher than when Reagan took office in 1981. This statistic alone has caused many critics to label the president's experiment with supply-side policies a miserable failure. It is an issue that will demand an increasing amount of the president's time during the remainder of his term. The unemployment rate is unlikely to fall rapidly regardless of public policy, since most projections indicate a slow recovery from the recession.

While the president may believe that public policy can do very little to reduce short-run unemployment, the magnitude of the present problem will force him to take policy action. The economic hardships created by long-term unemployment eventually will be translated into political or social unrest. Loss of family savings, homes, and other assets also carries a frustration and anger that will be directed toward political authorities. And since the president's economic program is viewed as a major cause of the problem, the president must respond with a positive employment program.

During the 1982 election campaign the president repeatedly asked voters to elect Republicans to Congress who would support his program. Reagan asked for additional time, arguing that a return to the policies of the past would bring renewed inflation and even greater economic problems. His plea was to "stay the course." His economic recovery program had set the nation on the course to recovery; it simply needed more time to succeed.

The November 1982 election was not a resounding repudiation of Reaganomics, although the president and the Republicans lost twenty-six House seats to the Democrats. The election was a mixed bag, since some Reagan supporters won and some were defeated, and many Republicans who won attempted to separate themselves from a hard-line stand in support of the president's policies. While both parties claimed victory, it is clear that the president will not have the same level of support in the new Congress that he has had in the past.[1]

The election was clearly a message that voters want action on the employment problem. While many people do not want to return to the policies of the past, they also want adjustments made in the Reaganomics package. The other important issues such as Social Security, monetary policy, the deficit, and defense will be dominated by the unemployment issue.

As the president and Congress approach 1983, what are the policy options? The first would be to stay the course, convinced that in the long run the policies begun in the past two years will prove successful. Economic growth will occur as a result of rising business confidence and increased investment, and unemployment will begin to fall. Even the president must recognize this course as both economically and politically inadequate.

While a strict adherence to the 1981-82 course is unrealistic, many supporters of the president want only slight modifications to the program. For example, they argue that deep cuts in entitlements and defense, while raising some taxes, would control the deficit, lower interest rates, and stimulate capital investment. While such adjustments may gain the support of the president, they do not adequately address the short-run unemployment issue seen as critical by congressional Democrats.[2]

A second course would be to follow the hard-line supply-siders, who argue for a monetary policy lid on interest rates, an acceleration of the remaining Reagan tax cuts, movement to a flat-rate tax, and a monetary system tied to gold. The short-run key is the reduction of interest rates so the stimulative effects of the tax cuts can be realized. The long-run key is still seen as the stability provided only by a return to the gold standard.

A third course is that likely to be taken by more traditional liberals, including Speaker of the House Tip O'Neill and Senator Edward Kennedy. Such a course will probably include major cuts in the projected defense budget and few, if any, cuts in the entitlement programs. Liberals also favor a monetary policy targeted to interest rates rather than the current money supply policy. Emphasis will be placed on short-run job creation through public spending to ensure a stronger recovery.

A variation of the Democrat's program places emphasis on investment in bridges, roads, sewers, and other public services and an increase in public research and development spending to expand long-run growth through industry-government cooperation.

Whatever the outcome of the 1983 session of Congress, it is certain to contain adjustments, if not major structural change, to the Reagan program. Such changes are likely to make the recession and the unemployment problems more visible parts of Reaganomics. The president may argue that this trend is only a minor change in emphasis and the central parts of the economic recovery program remain intact. Since the original goal of the program was to reduce inflation, the president can also argue that he has had at least partial success.

Detractors of Reaganomics have already labeled it an unqualified failure. Supporters argue that the major parts of supply-side theory were never really implemented, or have not been given adequate time to reach their objectives. In either case, the impact of the Reaganomics experiment in public policy has been great, and a new Congress will now decide whether or not to stay the course.

NOTES

Chapter 1

1   John M. Keynes, *The General Theory of Employment, Interest, and Money* (New York: Harcourt, Brace and World, 1936). The literature on Keynesian theory and the resulting policy is extensive. However, one of the first attempts to explain the theory was made by Alvin Hansen in *A Guide to Keynes* (New York: McGraw-Hill, 1953), and *Monetary Theory and Fiscal Policy* (New York: McGraw-Hill, 1949).

2   An excellent detailed review of the policy developments of the 1930-1980 period is presented in Thomas Cargill and Gillian Garcia, *Financial Deregulation and Monetary Control* (Stanford: Hoover Press, 1982).

3   These and most other budget figures are taken from various annual issues of *The Economic Report of the President* (Washington, D.C.: Government Printing Office).

Chapter 2

1   See, for example, the address delivered by the president to a joint session of Congress on 18 February 1981, in which he presented his economic proposals.

2   Arthur Laffer and Jan P. Seymour, *The Economics of the Tax Revolt* (New York: Harcourt Brace Jovanovich, Inc., 1979); Jude Wanniski, *The Way the World Works* (New York: Basic Books, 1978); Paul Craig Roberts, "Caricatures of Tax-Cutting," *Wall Street Journal*, 24 April 1980; Roberts, "Supply-Side Economics," *Wall Street Journal*, 28 Feb. 1980.

3   For example, see Michael Kinsley, "Alms for the Rich," *The New Repub-
     lic*, 19 Aug. 1978, 19-26; Walter Heller, "The Kemp-Roth-Laffer Free
     Lunch," *Wall Street Journal*, 12 July 1978.

4   Arthur Laffer and Charles Kadlec, "The Point of Linking the Dollar to
     Gold," *Wall Street Journal*, 13 Oct. 1981; Lewis Lehrman, "The Means
     to Establishing Financial Order," *Wall Street Journal*, 18 Feb. 1981;
     Lehrman, "The Case for the Gold Standard," *Wall Street Journal*, 30 July
     1981.

5   Milton Friedman, "A Restatement of the Quantity Theory of Money," in
     Milton Friedman, ed., *Studies in the Quantity Theory of Money* (Chicago:
     University of Chicago Press, 1956); Milton Friedman, *A Program for
     Monetary Stability* (New York: Fordham University Press, 1959).

6   Milton Friedman and Anna Schwartz, *A Monetary History of the United
     States, 1867-1960* (Princeton: Princeton University Press, 1963); Milton
     Friedman and David Meiselman, "The Relative Stability of Monetary
     Velocity and the Investment Multiplier, 1897-1958," in *Stabilization Pol-
     icy*, Prepared for the Commission on Money and Credit (Englewood Cliffs,
     N.J.: Prentice Hall, 1963).

7   For a more detailed theoretical description of rational expectations see
     Thomas Sargent and Neil Wallace, "Rational Expectations and the The-
     ory of Economic Policy," *Journal of Monetary Economics*, April 1976;
     William Poole, "Rational Expectations in the Macro Model," *Brookings
     Papers on Economic Activity*, 1976, 2d ed.

     For a less theoretical description, see Mark Willes, "The Rational Expec-
     tations Model," *Wall Street Journal*, 2 April 1979; Charles Plosser and
     Clifford Smith, "The People Can't Be Fooled," *Wall Street Journal*, 25
     June 1979; Clarence Nelson, "Rational Expectations—Fresh Ideas that
     Challenge Some Established Views of Policy Making," (1977 Annual Re-
     port, Federal Reserve Bank of Minneapolis).

8   Milton Friedman, "Nobel Lecture: Inflation and Unemployment," *Jour-
     nal of Political Economy*, June 1977, 451-72.

Chapter 3

1   Richard Goode, *The Individual Income Tax*, rev. ed. (Washington, D.C.:
     Brookings Institution, 1976), 3.

2   John Mueller, "Lessons of the Tax-Cuts of Yesteryear," *Wall Street Journal*, 5 March 1981.

3   Walter Heller, "The Kemp-Roth-Laffer Free Lunch," *Wall Street Journal*, 12 July 1978.

4   Mueller, "Lessons of the Tax-Cuts," *Wall Street Journal*, 5 March 1981.

5   *H.R. 16648*, 93d Cong., 2d sess.

6   Jack Kemp, Speech to Congress, 12 Nov. 1975, 94th Cong., 1st sess.

7   Heller, "The Kemp-Roth-Laffer Free Lunch," *Wall Street Journal*, 12 July 1978.

8   Jude Wanniski, "It's Time to Cut Taxes," *Wall Street Journal*, 11 Dec. 1974.

9   Arthur Laffer and Charles Kadlec, *The Jarvis-Gann Tax Cut Proposal: An Application of the Laffer Curve* (Boston: H.C. Wainwright and Co., 1978).

10   Walter Heller, "Meat-Axe Radicalism in California," *Wall Street Journal*, 5 June 1978.

11   "California's Phony Crisis," *Wall Street Journal*, 19 Jan. 1981.

12   Tom Hazlett, "Whatever Happened to Proposition 13?" *Readers Digest*, Sept. 1981, 124-27.

13   Marilyn Chase, "California's Public Services Suffer from Tax-Revolt Spending Cuts," *Wall Street Journal*, 16 Feb. 1982.

Chapter 4

1   "America's New Beginning: A Program for Economic Recovery" (Press Release from the White House, 18 Feb. 1981).

2   "Tax Cuts: How You Will Be Better Off," *U.S. News and World Report*, 10 Aug. 1981, 20-24.

3   "Those Budget Cuts—Who'll Be Hit Hardest," *U.S. News and World Report*, 10 Aug. 1981, 45-48.

4 "Tax Cuts," *U.S. News and World Report*, 10 Aug. 1981.

5 "Life After Death for 'Safe Harbor'," *Business Week*, 8 Nov. 1982, 105.

6 "Those Budget Cuts," *U.S. News and World Report*, 10 Aug. 1981.

7 "The Reagan Budget," *San Francisco Chronicle*, 7 Feb. 1982.

Chapter 5

1 Michael Evans, "The Source of Personal Saving in the U.S.," *Wall Street Journal*, 23 March 1981.

2 "Reaganomics' Effect on Savings," *Business Week*, 8 March 1982, 60-62.

Chapter 6

1 "Layoffs Signal a Slump that Will Not End Soon," *Business Week*, 30 Nov. 1981, 47-50.

2 "Reaganomics Races the Clock," *Business Week*, 30 Nov. 1981, 48-49.

3 Ralph Winter, "Business Leaders Begin to Express Skepticism about Reaganomics," *Wall Street Journal*, 29 Jan. 1982.

4 "The Housing Recession," *Business Week*, 21 Sept. 1981, 85.

5 "Reaganomics Races the Clock," *Business Week*, 30 Nov. 1981, 48-49.

   "Standing Pat on Reaganomics," *U.S. News and World Report*, 16 Nov. 1981, 24.

6 "Reaganomics' Effect on Savings," *Business Week*, 8 March 1982, 60-62.

7 "Why Savings May Stay High," *Business Week*, 13 Sept. 1982, 62.

8 "Far from Recovery in Capital Spending," *Business Week*, 12 July 1982, 21.

9 "Business Disappoints Congress," *Business Week*, 21 Dec. 1981, 36.

10   "Executives Still Support Reaganomics," *Business Week*, 26 April 1982, 20.

11   William Greider, "The Education of David Stockman," *Atlantic Monthly*, Dec. 1981, 27-54.

Chapter 7

1   "Will U.S. Treasury Hog Credit Market?" *U.S. News and World Report*, 19 July 1982, 72.

2   "The Search for a New Policy," *Business Week*, 8 Nov. 1982, 108-112.

3   "Budget-Cutting Makes a Checkered Impact," *Business Week*, 14 June 1982, 29.

4   "Biting the Bullet on Social Security," *U.S. News and World Report*, 8 Nov. 1982, 43-44.

5   See a summary of the proposal in "A Way to Save Social Security," Michael Boskin, John Shoven, Laurence Kotlikoff, *Business Week*, 8 Nov. 1982, 13.

6   "The Budget Scam," *Wall Street Journal*, 13 Aug. 1982.

7   Richard McKenzie, "An Introduction to the Personal Tax 'Cuts'," *Wall Street Journal*, 8 Jan. 1982.

     This point is examined thoroughly in Stephen Meyer and Robert Rossana, "Did the Tax Cut Really Cut Taxes?" International Institute for Economic Research, Reprint Paper 17, June 1982.

8   "Tax Squeeze: What It Means to You," *U.S. News and World Report*, 30 Aug. 1982, 18-22.

9   Susan Lee, "Rating the Flat-Rate Tax," *Wall Street Journal*, 30 June 1982.

10   For example, see Phillip Stern, *The Great Treasury Raid* (New York: Random House, 1964).

11   William Greider, "The Education of David Stockman," *Atlantic Monthly*, Dec. 1981, 27-54.

12   Ibid., 46.

13   Ibid., 32.

14   Ibid., 40.

15   Ibid., 39.

16   "Reaganomics: The Second Dose," *Federationist*, Feb. 1982, 11.

17   Walter Mossberg, "Problems With the Reagan Defense Budget," *Wall Street Journal*, 2 March 1982.

18   "Reagan's Blueprint for Shrinking Government," *Business Week*, 15 Feb. 1982, 134.

19   "Reaganomics: The Second Dose," *Federationist*, Feb. 1982, 90.

20   *Economic Report of the President, January 1983* (Washington, D.C.: Government Printing Office).

21   Paul Blustein, "Supply-Side Theories Became Federal Policy With Unusual Speed," *Wall Street Journal*, 8 Oct. 1981.

22   Roy Jastram, "The Gold Standard: You Can't Trust Politics," *Wall Street Journal*, 11 Nov. 1980.

23   Ibid.

24   Lewis Lehrman, "The Means to Establishing Financial Order," *Wall Street Journal*, 18 Feb. 1981.

25   "A Return to the Gold Standard," *Business Week*, 21 Sept. 1981, 114-20.

26   Robert Mundell, "Gold Would Serve into the 21st Century," *Wall Street Journal*, 30 Sept. 1981.

Chapter 8

1   "How Policy Will Change to Spur the Economy," *Business Week*, 15 Nov. 1982, 32-34.

2   "The Search for a New Policy," *Business Week*, 8 Nov. 1982, 108-112.

INDEX

†